Native American Chiefs and Warriors

By Stuart A. Kallen

Lucent Books
P.O. Box 289011, San Diego, CA 92198-9011

Other Books in the History Makers Series:

Artists of the Renaissance

Civil War Generals of the Confederacy

Civil War Generals of the Union

Fighters Against American Slavery

Leaders of Ancient Greece

Rulers of Ancient Egypt

Rulers of Ancient Rome

Scientists of Ancient Greece

Women of the American Revolution

Women Leaders of Nations

Library of Congress Cataloging-in-Publication Data

Kallen, Stuart A., 1955–
    Native American Chiefs and Warriors / by Stuart A. Kallen.
       p.   cm. — (History makers)
    Includes bibliographical references and index.
    Summary: Discusses the lives and achievements of five famous and
influential Native American chiefs: King Philip, Chief Pontiac, Geronimo,
Crazy Horse, and Wilma Mankiller.
    ISBN 1-56006-364-5 (lib. : alk. paper)
    1. Indians of North America—Kings and rulers—Biography—
Juvenile literature. [1. Indians of North America—Kings and rulers.
2. Indians of North America—Biography.] I. Title. II. Series.
E89.K35   1999
973'.0497'00922—dc21
[B]   99-13227
                                                                CIP
                                                                AC

CONTENTS

FOREWORD

The literary form most often referred to as "multiple biography" was perfected in the first century A.D. by Plutarch, a perceptive and talented moralist and historian who hailed from the small town of Chaeronea in central Greece. His most famous work, *Parallel Lives*, consists of a long series of biographies of noteworthy ancient Greek and Roman statesmen and military leaders. Frequently, Plutarch compares a famous Greek to a famous Roman, pointing out similarities in personality and achievements. These expertly constructed and very readable tracts provided later historians and others, including playwrights like Shakespeare, with priceless information about prominent ancient personages and also inspired new generations of writers to tackle the multiple biography genre.

The Lucent History Makers series proudly carries on the venerable tradition handed down from Plutarch. Each volume in the series consists of a set of six to eight biographies of important and influential historical figures who were linked together by a common factor. In *Rulers of Ancient Rome*, for example, all the figures were generals, consuls, or emperors of either the Roman Republic or Empire; while the subjects of *Fighters Against American Slavery*, though they lived in different places and times, all shared the same goal, namely the eradication of human servitude. Mindful that politicians and military leaders are not (and never have been) the only people who shape the course of history, the editors of the series have also included representatives from a wide range of endeavors, including scientists, artists, writers, philosophers, religious leaders, and sports figures.

Each book is intended to give a range of figures—some well known, others less known; some who made a great impact on history, others who made only a small impact. For instance, by making Columbus's initial voyage possible, Spain's Queen Isabella I, featured in *Women Leaders of Nations*, helped to open up the New World to exploration and exploitation by the European powers. Unarguably, therefore, she made a major contribution to a series of events that had momentous consequences for the entire world. By contrast, Catherine II, the eighteenth-century Russian queen, and Golda Meir, the modern Israeli prime minister, did not play roles of global impact; however, their policies and actions significantly influenced the historical development of both their own countries and their regional neighbors. Regardless of their relative importance in the greater historical scheme, all of the figures chronicled in the History Makers series made contributions to posterity; and their public achievements, as well as what is known about their private lives, are presented and evaluated in light of the most recent scholarship.

In addition, each volume in the series is documented and substantiated by a wide array of primary and secondary source quotations. The primary source quotes enliven the text by presenting eyewitness views of the times and culture in which each history maker lived; while the secondary source quotes, taken from the works of respected modern scholars, offer expert elaboration and/ or critical commentary. Each quote is footnoted, demonstrating to the reader exactly where biographers find their information. The footnotes also provide the reader with the means of conducting additional research. Finally, to further guide and illuminate readers, each volume in the series features photographs, two bibliographies, and a comprehensive index.

The History Makers series provides both students engaged in research and more casual readers with informative, enlightening, and entertaining overviews of individuals from a variety of circumstances, professions, and backgrounds. No doubt all of them, whether loved or hated, benevolent or cruel, constructive or destructive, will remain endlessly fascinating to each new generation seeking to identify the forces that shaped their world.

Native American Leaders

As the United States begins the twenty-first century, the days of cowboys and Indians seem far in the past. But it was little more than one hundred years ago that Native Americans fought with the U.S. Army over rights to land—land that was once entirely the domain of America's indigenous people. Although those final battles were fought in the Great Plains states of Montana, Wyoming, and the Dakotas, indigenous Native Americans have been fighting for their way of life since the Pilgrims first landed on American shores in the 1600s.

Many of those battles went unrecorded—Native Americans fought white people for three hundred years. During those three centuries, however, leaders appeared on the scene who rallied their people, won many battles, and became famous in their own time. Some of those Native American leaders are still held in high esteem today.

Although white people have always called these leaders "chief," the term is not one that was used by Native Americans. The word

Native Americans square off against colonists, foreshadowing nearly three hundred years of discord between whites and Indians.

chief implies an authority that few Indian leaders possessed, and the majority of chiefs led their people by consensus, not coercion.

Lakota Sioux chief Luther Standing Bear voices his opinion on this matter in his autobiography, *Land of the Spotted Eagle:*

> The common conception of a chief is that of a man who has great power, even power over life, and that he exerts his cruel might upon any and every pretext. And this idea, though far from the truth, has made of chiefs, blood thirsty and cruel savages, while as a matter of fact most of them were bene-factors of their people and were men who gave their best abilities, even sacrificed, to be of service to their fellows.
>
> No Lakota chief ever dreamed of using the power of a judge in court, or a policeman on a street corner. . . . No chief could declare warfare and command other braves to follow him. Neither could he declare war and remain at home, for to do so would have been to bring about his own ignominious destruction.[1]

Most tribes had many chiefs, each with different responsibilities. The Cheyenne, whose numbers never exceeded four thousand, had forty-four chiefs—four for each of the tribe's ten bands and four head chiefs. These men formed a governing council that decided major issues such as waging war, making alliances with neighbors, and moving camp to pursue buffalo.

Chiefs were usually picked on the basis of their intelligence, survival skills, or personal charisma. In some tribes chiefs were selected only by the female members, and if the women felt the chief was not doing a good job, he could be removed from office. A few tribes along the Atlantic Coast and in New England had female chiefs. In the 1980s and 1990s, Wilma Mankiller was the first female chief of the Cherokee in modern times.

It was the job of the tribal leader to keep his or her people safe, settle disputes between families, and ensure that care was provided for widows, the elderly, and orphans. Many chiefs were known for their generosity, and some of those who rose to leadership positions gave away food, horses, and trade goods in order to spread influence beyond their immediate clan.

War Chiefs

Although some chiefs led in war and in peace, most tribes had different leaders during times of war. Those leaders were chosen for their warrior skills, their grasp of military tactics, and for exhibiting

To achieve the rank of war chief, a Native American warrior had to possess an unsurpassed knowledge of warfare tactics and display the utmost bravery in battle.

exceptional bravery on the field of battle. Young men might try to show such abilities by stealing horses from an enemy camp, leading a successful war party, seizing their enemy's weapons in combat, or being the first to touch, or "count coup," upon an enemy, thereby humiliating the foe.

Native American war chiefs were not like leaders in the U.S. army. Indians did not have absolute power by virtue of rank or title; they led by reputation. Successful feats of daring added to a leader's stature, but the loss of even one warrior in battle might end a man's career as chief.

Every Native American tribe has its share of celebrated leaders. Since Native Americans did not have a written language, however, the stories of some chiefs have been changed and embellished over the years. Others remain shrouded in mystery. This issue is explored further in *The Mighty Chieftains:*

> Written history began only with the arrival of the Europeans, who chronicled the three-centuries-long white-Indian conflict that ended with the total military defeat of the Indian peoples. In tribe after tribe, this era of crisis called forth chiefs of heroic proportions.
>
> Against impossible odds, some conducted unrelenting warfare; others turned their energies to seek peace and ac-

commodation. All of them were patriots. For the most part, however, the greatness of these men was rarely recognized until after they were dead or no longer posed a threat to American expansion. King Philip, Pontiac . . . Geronimo . . . and Crazy Horse were reviled in their time as "savages," "bandits," and "threats to civilization." But the accounts of their lives reveal qualities well worth emulation—qualities that without a doubt descended through countless generations of Native American people—loyalty, bravery, wisdom, and dedication to improving the lot of their people.[2]

The chiefs whose lives are detailed in this book—King Philip, Pontiac, Crazy Horse, Geronimo, and Wilma Mankiller—came from four separate regions. King Philip, a Wampanoag, was from the northeast woodlands of modern-day New England. Pontiac, an Ottawa, was from the Great Lakes region. Crazy Horse, an Oglala Sioux, spent his entire life on the buffalo grounds of the Great Plains. Geronimo, an Apache, lived in the arid mountains and deserts of Arizona. Wilma Mankiller, a twentieth-century Cherokee chief, grew up on a reservation in Oklahoma. Although all of these chiefs were separated by time and distance, their battles to keep their people free make them noteworthy now and for generations to come.

CHAPTER 1

The First Americans

At the dawn of the seventeenth century, few human beings inhabited the vast expanse of America; perhaps 5 to 10 million Native Americans occupied the land. Some regions averaged less than one person per square mile. This low ratio of people to land provided plenty of game and other natural resources to support the small bands of Native Americans who were living in villages scattered throughout the forests, plains, and mountains.

This situation changed dramatically when English settlers arrived on American shores. The *Mayflower* brought 120 Pilgrims in 1620. By 1670—only fifty years later—as many as 40,000 people were living in the area where the Pilgrims first landed. By 1700 over 1.6 million people were living in New England.

The rapid influx of white people onto Native American lands was the same elsewhere. In 1790 only 4,300 whites were settled in the Ohio territories. By 1800 that number was 45,000. That same year more than 700,000 white settlers lived west of the Appalachian Mountains, where only twenty years earlier there had been none. By that time more than 100 million acres of Native American land had been transferred to white people. Between 1800 and 1880 the population of the United States jumped from 5 million to 50 million.

When the East Coast became crowded, the white settlers moved to the Midwest. It did not take too many years before that area was filled with farmhouses, factories, and towns. By the 1850s white settlers were moving ever farther west, crossing the Great Plains on their way to Oregon, Washington, and California.

In *Crazy Horse: The Strange Man of the Oglalas,* author Mari Sandoz describes the impression Native Americans had as this trickle of humanity turned into a tide crossing Sioux territory:

> The drowsy heat of middle August lay heavy as a furred robe on the Upper Country of the Shell River. . . . No rain came to lay the dust of the emigrant road. . . .

[The] trail had started, with just a little stream of white men coming through, and the Indian lifted his hand in welcome and went out to smoke and watch this lengthening village of the whites that moved past him day after day all summer, always headed in the same direction. He wondered that he never saw them come back, yet they must be the same ones each year, for there could not be that many people on all the earth. At first he wondered at the women and children too, for he had long thought of the whites as only men, although he had heard stories of the families that had been seen, the women with the pale, sick skins and the break-in-two bodies, the young ones pale too, with hair light and soft as the flying seed of the cottonwood that tickles the nose in summer.[3]

Although some Native Americans could not believe that so many people existed on the earth, the white people continued to arrive in Indian country. In every single area where the white settlers and explorers traveled, they clashed with the Native Americans who considered these regions their ancestral homelands. Fights with settlers led to battles with the U.S. Army and the predictable results. When the Native Americans lost the wars, they were forced to sign treaties and move onto reservations.

White settlers hoping to claim land in the untamed wilds of Oklahoma had little regard for the Native American tribes that inhabited the territory.

11

Tribes of North America

When French and English settlers first arrived in North America in the 1600s, scores of Native American tribes practiced a highly developed culture. The tribes each shared common beliefs and were governed by chiefs and leaders called sachems. Each tribe practiced its own form of spiritualism, but all had a deeply ingrained religious sense based on the worship of spirits in the natural world. They sustained themselves through agriculture, fishing, hunting, and gathering, and their ancestral homeland was the huge area that stretched from the Atlantic Coast to the Pacific Coast and from the frozen tundra north of the Great Lakes to the burning deserts of northern Mexico.

Most of these tribes simply called themselves "the People." Former Cherokee chief Wilma Mankiller discusses tribal names in her autobiography *Mankiller: A Chief and Her People:*

> The names by which many tribes are known today were given to them by white explorers and trappers. For example, Nez Percé, is a French phrase meaning "those with pierced noses." But the Nez Percés called themselves *Nimipu,* meaning "the People." The Iroquois, the Delawares, and the Pawnees all called themselves by names that also meant "the People," or "Real People."[4]

Life for the people of the eastern and southern woodlands in the 1600s depended on the rhythms of the changing seasons.

Native American Tribes

In the spring the Wampanoag ancestors of King Philip in New England would take to the woods to tap maple trees for maple sugar. After the sugaring season, women, carrying their babies on their backs in cradle boards, farmed communal fields growing maize (corn), squash, peas, beans, melons, and pumpkins.

Throughout the summer wild berries such as gooseberries, raspberries, blueberries, and a host of others were cooked into a paste and spread over sheets of birch bark. The sun then dried the paste into small thin cakes which the women tied in bundles for storage. Women harvested the crops in the fall and preserved the food for the coming winter. They ground corn into flour and dried squash and pumpkins in the sun.

In the fall migrating geese and ducks filled the skies. Hunters would shoot down the waterfowl and later smoke their meat. As the nights grew colder and the days shorter, Native American families packed up their possessions and left their summer fields for the winter hunt. Only the sick or very old remained behind in villages. The rest moved south to live in tepees (also spelled teepees or tipis) while hunting and trapping deer, buffalo, beavers, otters, foxes, and raccoons.

Typical tribes, such as Chief Pontiac's Ottawa, lived in loose networks of villages spread throughout their sovereign hunting grounds. The villages were generally located in meadows along riverbanks, where groups of up to twelve families lived in pole-and-bark buildings called longhouses. The roofs of these buildings possessed gaping holes so that smoke could escape from smoldering cooking and heating fires within. Low doorways were covered with animal skins.

Each tribe was divided into clans, and each clan had its own animal symbol, called a totem, which was painted above the door. Totems in the Seneca tribe, for example, were named the Bear, the Wolf, the Beaver, the Turtle, the Deer, the Snipe, the Heron, or the Hawk.

In the eastern tribes—and indeed in every Native American tribe—there were people who had gifts of healing or prophecy and were called shamans or medicine men. There were many different kinds, each with his own specialty. Some used knowledge of herbs to cure the sick. Other shamans performed healing rites using masks. Still others used magic stones, bones, and other items to predict the future, locate game, or find missing persons. The skills of medicine men were impressive. The therapeutic properties of certain plants were well known and used effectively.

The Plains Tribes

The tribes who roamed the Great Plains farther to the west were hard-riding warriors and hunters who were relative newcomers to the region. Most of the tribes, such as the Sioux, Comanche, Pawnee, Cheyenne, and Blackfoot, arrived in the region only after the thirteenth century.

The range of the Plains Indians extended from present-day North and South Dakota through Montana, Wyoming, Nebraska, Kansas, Oklahoma, and Texas. Their eastern border was the Mississippi River, and their western border was the Rocky Mountains. Although there were trees along riverbanks, the majority of the area was covered with a vast plateau of short-grass prairie—perfectly suited to the grazing needs of 30 to 50 million buffalo.

Rainfall in the Great Plains rarely exceeded ten inches a year, but fertile forests of oak, elm, willow, and cottonwood graced the banks of the Missouri, Platte, Arkansas, and Kansas Rivers as well as their tributaries. These woods sustained early Native Americans in the area with a wealth of game, including bears, deer, antelopes, rabbits, fish, and waterfowl.

Centuries before white people ever came to the region, a number of nomadic tribes scraped out a sparse living hunting buffalo. Because these tribes knew nothing of farming, the hunt was a matter of life and death. And hunting was conducted on foot—the horse was not introduced to the region until the late seventeenth century. (Although the Spanish explorer Francisco Vásquez de Coronado brought horses to the grasslands in 1541, they were not common until the 1700s.)

By the 1300s new bands began to move into the Great Plains from the east and west. These newcomers were farmers and ranchers, and they taught the nomadic tribes the rudiments of farming. They lived near rivers in lodges built of logs and covered with layers of dirt and grass much like the sod houses later built by white settlers. In the spring, after the crops were planted, entire villages left their homes to hunt buffalo. During this time, they lived in buffalo-skin tepees in hunting camps near the herds. There, the men hunted the huge animals with bows and arrows or stampeded herds off cliffs.

The Horse Culture

The simple farming lives of the Oglala ancestors of Crazy Horse and other Plains Indians were changed drastically when horses made their way into the region. On horseback, hunters could weave and dart throughout the buffalo herd and engage in raids on other tribes. In the past they only left their villages for a few weeks a year, but now the tribes returned home only to plant crops in the spring and stay sheltered in the winter.

The Sacred Buffalo

The Indians of the Great Plains treated the buffalo both as a sacred animal and as a good provider of all necessities. Buffalo meat, considered far superior to beef, was roasted, dried, and made into soup. The liver was a delicacy eaten by the hunter immediately after the kill. After the meat was taken, the Plains people used every other part that remained. Bones were whittled into needles, and sinew (tendon) was rolled into thread. These items were used to sew buffalo bladders into water bags and buffalo hide into clothing, drums, lassos, and bridles. Large buffalo leg bones were formed into knives, awls, and scrapers, and hooves were boiled into glue. Ribs and jawbones were used for sleds, which could be used for child's play or to transport goods through the snow. Spoons and cups were made from buffalo horn. Children collected dried buffalo dung to feed campfires. Sixteen to twenty buffalo hides were sewn together to make tepees, the portable cone-shaped tents that housed Sioux families.

There may have been as many as 30 to 50 million buffalo roaming the Great Plains when the white settlers first arrived. To eradicate the Indians, army officers encouraged hunters to kill buffalo on native lands. They correctly assumed that the slaughter of the buffalo would starve the natives and force them onto reservation land. According to author Benjamin Capps in *The Great Chiefs*, General Philip Sheridan praised buffalo hunters for "destroying the Indian's commissary. For the sake of lasting peace, let them kill, skin, and sell until they have exterminated the buffalo. Then your prairies will be covered with speckled cattle and the festive cowboy."

The U.S. Army encouraged white hunters to kill buffalo to cut off the Indians' food supply.

By the time a Plains Indian child was four or five years old, he or she owned a pony. As the child grew, he or she practiced a wide range of riding tricks and skills. Indian horses were known for their agility, speed, and endurance. They responded instantly to touch or word, and they were bred by their owners to possess

With the aid of their agile steeds, Great Plains warriors maneuver through a buffalo herd during the spring hunt.

great form and intelligence. In later years some tribes would own as many as fifteen thousand horses, and some war chiefs personally owned over one thousand horses each.

The Great Plains tribes formed military societies, each of which played an important part of tribal life. These groups guarded the camps, preserved order during tribal hunts, and practiced war. They also gave feasts, held games, and passed down tribal lore from generation to generation.

The dominance of the Great Plains tribes was spectacular but short lived. The white man's horse had made a rich life possible, but the white man himself brought a bloody end to the people of the Great Plains by the end of the nineteenth century.

Native Americans of the Southwest

Farther to the south and west of the Great Plains lived tribes such as the Apache, who were cunningly adapted to a way of life in a harsh land. Their ancestral homelands of mesas, deserts, canyons, and buttes suffered extremes in temperature. Deserts might reach 110 degrees in the summer and the snow-covered mountains 10 degrees in the winter. The tribes, however, drew sacred power from the red, brown, and purple bluffs that surrounded them. As the Apache chief Geronimo once said, "There is food everywhere if one only knows how to find it."[5]

Before the Spanish brought horses to the area, Apache men hunted wearing animal-head masks in order to sneak up on bighorn sheep, antelope, and deer. Women fed their families with wild plants, nuts, and seeds. The most important food source was the nutritious root of the spiky mescal plant, which was harvested each July, roasted in pits, sun dried, and transported back to camp in pack trains.

Although some tribes in the Southwest, such as the Navajo, were farmers, the Apache and others were nomadic. Their wanderings brought them in contact with many different native peoples, and they adopted the customs and practices of many of those peoples. For centuries, however, the Apache zealously maintained their reputation as ferocious raiders and warriors. They hit their enemies hard and often, looting and killing without remorse. Their lifestyles are explored in *America's Fascinating Indian Heritage:*

> Loosely organized into bands of hunters and raiders, all Apache tribes or groupings shared a common language. But the cultural traits they came to exhibit varied widely from band to band depending, in large measure, on the particular region each group roamed and the customs they borrowed from the peoples with whom they had contact.[6]

The Jicarilla Apache were buffalo hunters who farmed occasionally. The Lipan Apache engaged solely in hunting and gathering in eastern New Mexico and western Texas. War chief Geronimo's tribe, the Chiricahua Apache, were the fiercest raiders of all and lived by capturing horses, cows, and sheep raised by others.

The European Influence

Native American tribes had the North American continent to themselves for thousands of years. But the dominance of the tribes began to crumble in the seventeenth century, when French, English, and Dutch settlers arrived on the East Coast. From Virginia to New York to Maine, the influence the whites had on the Indians was about the same and had the same sad end. The white settlers introduced guns, diseases, and alcohol to the Native Americans. In turn, they took Native American lands starting on the East Coast and moving steadily to the West.

When whites supplied guns to one tribe but not another, formerly weak tribes were able to fight and conquer their enemies, forcing them from their traditional lands. These refugee tribes then fled to the lands of other tribes, causing more conflict. The balance of power between tribes, which had been maintained for centuries, was suddenly thrown into chaos.

The Europeans also brought with them a host of trade goods, including iron cookware, knives, sewing needles, and cloth. The Native Americans readily accepted these items which made their lives much easier. Within two or three generations, however, the cultures lost the skills needed to make this equipment using their traditional methods and materials. As these abilities faded, the Native Americans became totally dependent on trade with white people to maintain their lifestyles.

The introduction of guns and trade goods was a small problem when compared to the diseases that the whites introduced. Native Americans had few antibodies in their blood to fight the deadly illnesses that the Europeans brought with them from across the sea. These diseases included smallpox, influenza, measles, whooping cough, scarlet fever, diphtheria, yellow fever, typhoid fever, and meningitis. Although these diseases also killed white people, they had a devastating effect on Native Americans, sometimes killing more than half of an entire tribe.

Clash of Cultures

More than anything, the hostilities between the Europeans and the Native Americans was a clash of cultures. White people believed that one person could own a piece of land and that person could do whatever he or she wanted with it. Native Americans, however, believed that the land belonged to the spirits of the animals who lived on it. Luther Standing Bear elaborates:

> From Wakan Tanka [the Great Spirit] there came a great unifying life force that flowed through all things—the flowers of the plains, blowing wind, rocks, trees, birds, animals—this was the same force that had been breathed into the first man. Thus all things were kindred and brought together by the same Great Mystery. . . .
>
> The animal had rights—the right of man's protection, the right to live, the right to multiply, the right to freedom, the right to man's indebtedness. . . . Everything was possessed of personality, only differing from us in form. . . . The world was a library and its books were the stones, leaves, grass, brooks, and the birds and animals that shared alike with us.[7]

White people seemed afraid of the wilderness, and Native Americans had a difficult time understanding both the fear and the desire to tame it. "Many times the Indian is embarrassed and baffled by the white man's allusions to nature in terms such as

Native Americans and Alcohol

Europeans brought many prized commodities to trade with the Native Americans, including alcoholic beverages. Before the arrival of the Europeans, most Native Americans had absolutely no exposure to alcohol. Rum, brandy, beer, and wine had a strong effect on the Indians as liquor came into common use in villages. The destructive effects of liquor caused problems that Native Americans had never faced before. Drunken men quarreled with their wives and neighbors and conflicts sometimes ended in violence. Likewise, traders often plied Indians with alcohol to take advantage of them. As a result, alcoholism became a common disease.

In her autobiography Mankiller: A Chief and Her People, *Wilma Mankiller describes the devastation alcohol has caused her people.*

"In time, alcohol became even more ruinous than smallpox. When rum was introduced into the Appalachian Mountains, it was swapped to Indian tribes for deerskins. The impact of 'demon rum' on Native American societies brought catastrophic change to the world of the [Indians]."

Mankiller goes on to say that of the many factors that weakened her tribe, including warfare with the whites, alcoholism was one of the worst. She explains why many Indians turned to alcohol to try to relieve their pain.

"Cherokees and other native people no longer thought of themselves in any sort of compatible liaison with the world around them. Many Native Americans felt utterly violated and compromised. It seemed as if the spiritual and social tapestry they had created for centuries was unraveling. Everything lost that sacred balance. And ever since, we have been striving to return to the harmony we once had."

A frontiersman offers a bottle of alcohol to his Native American trading partner.

crude, primitive, wild, rude, untamed, and savage," says Standing Bear. For the Lakota, mountains, lakes, rivers, springs, valleys, and woods were all finished beauty."[8]

> We did not think of the great open plains, the beautiful rolling hills, and winding streams with tangled growth, as "wild." Only to the white man was nature a "wilderness," and only to him was the land "infested" with "wild" animals and savage people. To us it was tame. Earth was bountiful and we were surrounded with the blessings of the Great Mystery. Not until the hairy man from the east came and with brutal frenzy heaped injustices upon us and the families we loved was it wild for us. When the very animals of the forest began fleeing from his approach, then it was that for us the "Wild West" began.[9]

Treaties and Reservations

When Native Americans lost their battles with white armies, they were forced to negotiate treaties that ceded their land to the U.S. government and confined them to tiny reservations. The United States signed close to three hundred treaties with Native Americans between the late eighteenth and late nineteenth centuries. These treaties, put together by well-trained lawyers, were written in confusing legal language barely intelligible to the average white citizens who understood English. To the Native Americans who could not read English, the treaties were incomprehensible. Whatever the language, all treaties served one purpose: to legally transfer Native American lands to the federal government.

The reservations where Native Americans were forced to live were usually in harsh, inhospitable regions where no one else wanted to live. By the mid-1870s, these reservations were virtual prisons. They were ruled by corrupt Indian agents who had total power over the people who lived there. According to Alvin M. Josephy Jr. in *500 Nations,*

> Shut inside the reservations, where outside eyes could not see them, the Indian peoples were subjected to unspeakable abuses. Housing moneys were stolen, food rations were inadequate or spoiled, people were left to die without medical treatment or medicines, others were forcibly separated from their families to be punished without trial for real or trumped-up offenses, and individual Indians were frequently murdered. . . .

A nineteenth-century cartoon ridicules the deplorable state of early Indian reservations. Native Americans starved while corrupt Indian agents stockpiled wealth.

> Trapped on the reservations, without freedom and the ability to provide for themselves in time-tested fashion or make their complaints known, the Indian families lived in poverty and misery.[10]

Eventually government reformers became aware of white corruption on Indian reservations, but they determined that the only lasting solution was not to change the system but to change the Native Americans themselves. Indian traditions, beliefs, and ways of life were condemned as immoral. If Native Americans were to be "saved," they had to adopt white culture, manners, and religion.

In 1889 Thomas Jefferson Morgan, the government's commissioner of Indian affairs, expressed his convictions on what had to be done to save the Indians:

> The logic of events demands the absorption of the Indians into our national life, not as Indians but as American citizens. . . .

> The Indian must conform to "the white man's ways," peaceably if they will, forcibly if they must. They. . . must conform their mode of living substantially to our civilization.

This civilization may not be the best possible, but it is the best the Indians can get. They cannot escape it, and must either conform to it or be crushed by it.[11]

To enforce this policy, Native American rituals and sacred ceremonies were banned. Medicine men and shamans were arrested and jailed. Old traditions such as telling stories, singing, dancing, and speaking in tribal languages were also forbidden.

Special attention was given to educating the young, who were forcibly taken from their parents and sent to faraway schools off the reservations. The first "Indian school" was established in Carlisle, Pennsylvania, in 1879. Native American children from across the country were shipped there. Those who did not die from disease were taught academic and vocational trades. Luther Standing Bear was forced to leave the Pine Ridge Reservation in 1889 to go to Carlisle:

> I could think of no reason white people wanted Indian boys and girls except to kill them, and not having the remotest idea of what a school was, I thought we were going East to die. But so well had courage and bravery been trained into us that it . . . was nothing when it came time to do something for the tribe.[12]

An 1886 photograph shows a group of Apache children upon their arrival at the Carlisle Indian School.

The school, which lasted until 1918, inspired dozens of other Indian schools across the country.

The Dawes Act

In 1887 a group of eastern reformers and western land speculators pushed a law through Congress called the Dawes General Allotment Act, which broke up the communal land of the reservations into 160-acre plots to be assigned to individual Native Americans. Unscrupulous Indian agents signed the names of dogs and dead people to reservation rolls to obtain the 160-acre allotments.

According to the Dawes act, any acreage left over after each Native American received 160 acres could be sold to white people. The reformers meant to destroy the group-oriented Native American culture and replace it with independent, land-owning capitalism.

In 1887, before the passage of the Dawes act, Indian nations still held 138 million acres of land in the United States. By 1934, when the act ended, 95 million of those acres had been lost or sold to whites. Likewise, a large part of the remainder was under lease to whites. These developments occurred because many Native Americans were unable to adapt to farming and because much of the land was unsuitable to agriculture. More than ninety thousand Native Americans were left landless.

Today, because of treaties and Supreme Court decisions over the years, Indian nations have regained their status as autonomous nations—separate yet existing within the boundaries of the United States. A few tribes have opened casinos and bingo parlors and have made financial fortunes. Casino moneys have been used to fund schools, health care programs, and other services. Most reservations, however, remain much the same as they were during the nineteenth century—with high unemployment, substandard housing, and a host of other social problems.

In recent years, however, the Native American population has grown to some 2.5 million, up from only 245,000 at the turn of the nineteenth century. This resurgence is more than just numbers; Native Americans are renewing their determination to make their own destiny in a world much different from that of their ancestors.

Perhaps this conflict between the old ways and the new was best discussed in 1977 by a U.S. congressional committee called the American Indian Policy Review Commission. Its report summed up two hundred years of government policy toward Native Americans:

Casinos have generated immense profits for a small percentage of Native American tribes, enabling them to become more self-sufficient and to improve their quality of life.

From the earliest days of European settlement . . . the Indians have been subjected to . . . attitudes and policies by the advancing non-Indian society, and . . . by the United States Government itself. On one hand, every method has been employed to force them to cease being Indians and to conform to the dominant society, while on the other hand they have been led to believe . . . that the government would support their right to survive as Indians. . . . Today we must ask the central question: Is the American nation—now two hundred years old, and one hundred full years beyond the era of Little Big Horn—yet mature enough and secure enough to tolerate, even to encourage, within the larger culture, societies of Indian people who wish to maintain their own unique tribal governments, cultures, and religions?[13]

CHAPTER 2

King Philip

The beginning of Native American troubles goes back to the days when the first white people set foot on the shores of America. In the early seventeenth century Native Americans far outnumbered the handful of Europeans who were landing in modern-day New England. A few far-sighted chiefs, however, understood that these explorers and adventurers wanted more than just trade goods. The white people also wanted land— land they could farm, land they could mine, and land they could timber. They wanted ownership of this land, and they wanted to pass it down to their sons and daughters when they died.

Metacomet, the Wampanoag chief who would gain fame as King Philip, lived during the 1600s in modern-day Massachusetts and Rhode Island.

One of the chiefs who foresaw this threat to his people was Metacomet, a leader of the Wampanoag tribe. Metacomet was the second son of Massasoit, also known as Yellow Feather, who was a grand sachem—the chief of his tribe's ruling council.

Before the white settlers and traders came to North America, the Wampanoag tribe lived in much of present-day Rhode Island and southern Massachusetts, including Cape Cod and the islands of Martha's Vineyard and Nantucket. They inhabited an area with dozens of other Native American tribes, whose total numbers reached about fifty thousand according to modern estimates. All of these tribes spoke a variation of the Algonquian language but were distributed in various Indian nations, each with its own name and territory. These nations were made up of loosely associated tribes. Some of the tribes who lived near the Wampanoag included the Nipmuck, the Massachuset, and the Nauset.

The twenty-four thousand members of the Wampanoag tribe lived in separate villages consisting of a few hundred people. Their houses were called wigwams, and they were covered with bark, mats sewn of cattails, or woven bulrushes. Like many other Native American tribes, the Wampanoag moved their villages according to the seasons. They lived in different locations depending on whether they were farming, hunting, fishing, or camping for the winter. In the summer the Wampanoag tribe grew corn, beans, gourds, and tobacco. Women raised all of the crops except tobacco, which was used only by men.

The European Plague

Around 1616 European tradesmen and explorers unwittingly infected the Native Americans with a plague, which was most likely smallpox. This disease, to which Native Americans had little resistance, killed almost all of the Massachuset tribe and about two-thirds of the Wampanoag. The havoc wreaked by this unprecedented force in the wilderness was described by Thomas Morton, an Englishman who had visited the New World:

> The hand of God fell heavily upon [the Indians] with such a mortall stroake that they died on heapes, as they lay in their houses, and the living, that were able to shift for themselves would runne away and let them dy, and let there Carkases ly above the ground without buriall. For in a place where many inhabited, there hath been but one a live, to tell what became of the rest . . . they were left for the Crowes, Kites, and vermin to pray upon.[14]

Not everyone was saddened by this disaster. The plague left entire villages empty, leaving the land open for white settlement. In England, King James I hailed "the wonderful plague among the savages." An early colonist agreed with his king when he wrote, "By this meanes Christ . . . not onely made roome for his people to plant but also tamed the hard and cruell hearts of these barbarous Indians."[15]

For centuries the Wampanoag had successfully fought off other tribes who wanted their lands, such as the Narraganset, or "the People of the Point," who lived along the Rhode Island coast. But

Abundance of Food

The staple foods of King Philip's tribe were corn, kidney beans, and squash. Women prepared the corn by simply boiling it with the beans. They also ground parched corn into flour and baked it into *nokake,* a cake that warriors ate on hunting expeditions.

The Wampanoag believed that the supreme god, Cautantowwit, was the provider of this food as well as the fish and game. Cautantowwit lived in the Southwest, where the warm weather originated. The crow was his messenger, and it flew from the Southwest with a kernel of corn and a bean in each ear. The crow dispersed the corn among the northern tribes. This gave the crow a special significance among animals, all of whom were sacred to Native Americans.

The Wampanoag believed that Cautantowwit would provide power, health, and food, and when they died, the Native Americans believed that their spirit would go to the Southwest, where it was endlessly warm and beautiful.

When a Wampanoag killed an animal while hunting, he performed a ritual to give thanks to the animal. When beavers were killed, for instance, the hunter would feed his family with the animal while his wife made clothes from the skin. The beaver's bones were saved, protected, and later returned to their native stream.

When the English first arrived in the area, they were amazed at the abundance of fish and game. They wrote about oceans teaming with smelt, alewives, and sturgeon. When the fish swam upstream to spawn, they were so abundant that it was possible to cross the stream on their backs. Within a century, however, overhunting and fishing by the whites seriously depleted dozens of native species.

Smoke rises from fires used for roasting and boiling fish. Wampanoag land once abounded with fish and game.

the one thousand or so Wampanoag survivors of the smallpox epidemic found their power threatened by their traditional Native American enemies. To improve his people's weakened circumstances, Massasoit offered a treaty of peace and friendship to the Puritan pilgrims who had settled nearby.

Massasoit (left) offers a peace pipe to the Puritan leaders, a gesture symbolizing their new alliance.

Conflict with the Puritans

The alliance forged between Massasoit and the Puritans benefited the whites for many years. In 1636, however, with no interference from the Wampanoag, the first Indian-white conflict in New England wiped out the Pequot tribe. In that battle, two hundred Puritans massacred seven hundred Pequot tribespeople. If Massasoit had sided with the Pequot, the united tribes might have driven the Puritans out of the New World. But Massasoit chose not to because the Pilgrims had earlier protected the Wampanoag from the Narraganset, and also supplied them with a steady supply of valuable trading goods.

The Wampanoag paid a price for dealing with the white people: Since the New England settlements were safe from Indian attack, more and more Puritans arrived from England. In addition to the English, settlers also came from the Netherlands, Germany, Italy, and Ireland. As coastal towns filled with people, land became scarce; white authorities soon demanded larger tracts of Wampanoag hunting grounds.

It was into this rapidly changing world that Metacomet was born in approximately 1638. The Wampanoag tribe kept no written records, but as Metacomet grew up he heard stories from his father and other elders. He learned that the Wampanoag had controlled their own destinies before the whites arrived.

When Metacomet reached adolescence, the lives of his family and his tribespeople were in a constant state of change as they struggled to both accommodate and resist the English. A skilled trader, Massasoit acted as a middleman between the Native Americans and the whites, which allowed him to amass great power and wealth. Young Metacomet lived a life of ease and material comfort, as did his older brother, Wamsutta, who was next in line to become the tribe's grand sachem.

The European Settlers

The Puritans were English pilgrims who were strictly religious people committed to lives based on the Bible. On September 16, 1620, 102 Pilgrims left England in a ship called the *Mayflower*. They landed on Cape Cod's Plymouth Rock on December 21. Because they had no legal right to settle in the region, they drew up the Mayflower Compact, creating their own government. Unlike Native Americans who considered religion a personal matter, the Puritans were inflexible. The church was the center of their lives. In their minds, the Indians were equal to the devil.

According to *So Dreadful a Judgment*, by Richard Slotkin and James Folsom, one of the Puritans' mandates in the New World was to "incite the Natives of [the] Country to the knowledge and obedience of the onlie true God and Savior of Mankind." To this end, a few missionaries tried to convert Native Americans to Christianity. These Indians were expected to cut their hair and work hard making baskets and brooms for the whites. Instead of sharing excess food, the natives were taught to sell it. Most important, Native Americans were expected to stop observing their native customs and completely sever all ties to their tribes. Because of this strict regimen, few Native Americans converted to Puritanism.

Massasoit's desire to have his children accepted by the Puritans led him to ask the Plymouth general court to give his sons English names. To Native Americans, names held supernatural powers. In fact, names were so personal that it was considered rude to call someone by his or her real name. Taking a new name had great meaning because it indicated the birth of a new person.

Court officials considered Massasoit the king of his people, so they chose distinguished names from ancient history for his sons. Wamsutta was called Alexander after Alexander the Great, the Macedonian king who conquered Greece around 300 B.C. Metacomet was renamed Philip after Philip II, the father of Alexander the Great.

In spite of his best efforts, Massasoit could not satisfy English demands for more land. The two cultures had vastly different views. According to *The Mighty Chieftains,*

> Many of the strict Puritans considered the Indians nothing more than agents of Satan and thus fair game for any ploy that might cause them to sign away their land. A [property] deed meant nothing to a Wampanoag, who believed in the right to hunt or grow crops on any land not in use. Some disputes went to colonial courts, where the judges sided with their fellow whites; others ended in violence, raising tempers on both sides.[16]

When Massasoit died at the age of eighty in 1661, Puritan authorities decided it was time to conquer and subordinate the Wampanoag. They ordered the new grand sachem, Alexander, to appear before them and promise to submit to the Puritan powers. Alexander resented what he felt was an encroachment of English power and refused to go. The authorities sent troops to forcibly bring Alexander to them.

Alexander fell ill with fever while undergoing harsh questioning. Wampanoag tribesmen came to carry him home, but the Puritans kept the grand sachem's two young sons as hostages. Alexander died before he could be returned to his village.

Court-Ordered Harassment

Although they could not prove it, the Wampanoag blamed Alexander's death on the English, and they rallied around their new grand sachem, Philip, the man the whites called King Philip. After a mourning ritual for Alexander was finished, ceremonies to honor Philip began. Night after night, Philip's village hosted dances and feasts. Leaders from tribes throughout the region came to pay their respects to the new sachem.

Native Americans from near and far gather to pay a tribute to Philip, the new grand sachem of the Wampanoag tribe.

By the time he was twenty-four years old, Philip had learned the gracious ways of a diplomat by observing the grand sachem Massasoit as he negotiated with the Puritans. And although Philip was known for his bravery and statesmanship, both would soon be tested by the colonial government.

In 1667, with its supply of public land nearly gone, the general court approved settlement at Swansea, located at the mouth of the Mount Hope peninsula in Rhode Island and the site of Philip's Sowam village. Settlers moved in and cut great swaths of forest to farm and built houses and a church. Tribesmen were arrested for hunting on "white" land. This invasion of settlers increased hostilities between the whites and the Wampanoag.

Tensions mounted further when authorities seized guns from the Wampanoag. Philip was summoned before the court to answer charges that he had been plotting to retake land from the settlers. The grand sachem protested that he was innocent and accused his Narraganset enemies of telling lies about him. The Plymouth government ignored Philip's defense and levied a fine of forty pounds against him. It relented on the issue of firearms, however, and returned the confiscated guns.

Smoldering Resentments

In 1671 Philip was again called before the court for plotting a Native American uprising. This time the authorities demanded that members of the Wampanoag tribe surrender their guns as a promise of good behavior. Surrounded by English soldiers, Philip had no choice but to turn seventy weapons over to the colonists. This act was detrimental to the Wampanoag because they needed their weapons to defend themselves against enemy tribes as well as to hunt.

The grand sachem began to seriously question his father's policy of appeasing the colonists. He gained new resolve to protect his people by any means and lost his will for diplomatic negotiation. It was all too clear that Massasoit's alliance with the settlers had done little good for the Wampanoag, who were losing their independence to the English.

Throughout the summer rumors of a Wampanoag war on white villages spread. King Philip was said to be organizing tribes friendly with the Wampanoag into a unified fighting force. When the rumors reached the authorities in Plymouth, Philip was once again summoned before the court.

On September 29, 1671, the grand sachem was forced to attend an inquest at the Plymouth general court with the governors of Massachusetts and Connecticut. Philip was ordered to relinquish his power as grand sachem. He was forced to sign a piece of paper that acknowledged full English authority over his tribe. From that day onward, his people would be subject to all of Plymouth's laws. As punishment for breaking the earlier agreement, he was fined one hundred pounds.

This sort of official harassment surely took its toll on Philip. According to the *Diary of King Philip's War, 1675–1676*, "We shall never know how the resentments of this proud man smoldered in the next three years but we can be sure he made plans for vengeance." [17]

Back in his village, Philip was accused of cowardice for giving in to the English demands. He countered that he never planned to comply to the treaty's demands. Philip clearly understood the threat that the English posed to his tribe. He believed giving in to their demands would drive his people to extinction. Plans to wage war were seriously discussed. If the Wampanoag were to have any hope of winning such a battle, all of New England's tribes would have to forge a united front.

Philip began a mission to create unity among the tribes, some of whose bitter rivalries dated back generations. From the main Wampanoag village of Pokanoket, Philip sent messengers to other tribes. The grand sachem personally attended distant tribal councils to convince reluctant leaders of the need for unity, but many chiefs felt it was too dangerous to take on such a formidable enemy as the English army.

For the next three years the anger continued to smolder between the Plymouth colonists and the Wampanoag. Neither side made any attempt to reconcile their differences.

Prelude to War

In the autumn of 1674 John Sassamon, a Native American who had converted to Christianity, began spying on the Wampanoag. In December he reported to authorities in Plymouth that Philip was planning to attack the town of Swansea. A month later Sassamon was found with a broken neck near his home. White officials used Sassamon's death as an excuse to take action against the Wampanoag. Three months later three of Philip's subchiefs were hanged for the murder following a one-sided trial attended by hundreds of angry settlers.

The executions infuriated the Wampanoag. When Philip demanded retribution from the authorities, they instead questioned him as to his involvement in Sassamon's murder. Philip's inability to obtain justice from the whites again called into question his role as leader of his people. A group of young aggressive warriors in his tribe initiated a two-week war dance. Shortly after, on June 20, 1675, the warriors ransacked the town of Swansea while the settlers were in church. No one was killed in this attack, but the whites were outraged to see their homes destroyed.

Philip's inability to obtain justice for the murder of fellow tribesmen led to a two-week war dance followed by all-out war with the whites.

John Easton, the deputy governor of Rhode Island, was a Quaker whose religious beliefs included nonviolence. Easton tried to head off a bloodbath by visiting Philip in his village. When the grand sachem met with the sympathetic Easton, he unleashed a torrent of complaints. These were dutifully written down by Easton, who referred to Philip and other Native American chiefs as kings. Philip's transcribed words were reprinted in the *Diary of King Philip's War, 1675–1676*. According to Easton,

[The Indians] said, they had been the first in doing good to the English, and the English the first in doing wrong; when the English first came, the king's father was as a great man, and the English as a little child; he constrained other Indians from wronging the English, and gave them corn and showed them how to plant, and was free to do them any good, and had let them have a hundred times more land than now the king had for his own people. But their king's brother [Alexander], when he was king, came miserably to die, by being forced to court, as [the Wampanoag] judge [he was] poisoned.

And another grievance was, if twenty of their honest Indians testified that an Englishman had done them wrong, it was as nothing; and if but one of their worst Indians testified against any Indian or their king, when it pleased the English, it was sufficient.

Another grievance was, when their kings sold land, the English would say it was more than they agreed to, and a writing must be proof against all of them; and some of their kings had done wrong to sell so much that they left their people none; and some being given to drunkenness the English made them drunk and then cheated them in bargains. Now their kings were forewarned not to part with land for nothing, in comparison to the value thereof. . . .

Another grievance, the English were so eager to sell the Indians liquors that most of the Indians spent all in drunkenness and then ravened upon the sober Indians and they did believe often did hurt English cattle, and their kings could not prevent it.[18]

Easton tried to convince the Wampanoag that war with the English was futile because the whites were too strong for them. The Native Americans reminded Easton that they were once a strong people and that they had helped the English. They believed the English owed them the same. Easton wrote that the Indians said, "Then the English should do for them as they did when they were too strong for the English." [19] Within a week, the settlers and the Wampanoag were at war.

The First Blood

After the raid at Swansea, most—but not all—of the settlers living in the area had abandoned their homesteads. Meanwhile, soldiers from Plymouth arrived and established their headquarters in a local reverend's house. Shortly afterward, an old white settler walking with a teenage boy saw three Native Americans near the abandoned homes at Swansea. According to *The First Frontier,*

> The old man bid the young man shoot, which he did, and one of the Indians fell down, but got away again. . . . [Later] some Indians came to the garrison and asked why they had shot the Indian. The men in the garrison asked whether he was dead. The Indians said yes. An English lad present said it was no matter. The men endeavored to inform them that it was but an idle lad's words, but the Indians went away in haste and did not listen to them. The next day the lad that shot the Indian, and his father, and five other English were killed. So the war began with Philip.[20]

The Native Americans exacted bloody justice, killing the boy who had shot one of their own. Other warriors attacked a group of Swansea whites who were returning from worship. One man was killed. That night two soldiers were shot dead and another two were mortally wounded. Two men were also shot who left to get medical aid; the following day their mutilated bodies were discovered by passing settlers.

More soldiers arrived in the area, and the army marched to Mount Hope in an attempt to trap the Native Americans on the peninsula. Not far from their encampment, the soldiers were fired on by a dozen Native Americans. One soldier died, two others were wounded. The Wampanoag warriors retreated, and the soldiers continued to Mount Hope. The Englishmen soon arrived at a place called Kickamuit, where, according to Benjamin Church in the *Diary of King Philip's War, 1675–1676,* the soldiers "took down the heads of eight Englishmen that were killed . . . and set upon poles, after the barbarous manner of those savages." [21] After burying the bodies, the soldiers found that Philip and the Wampanoag had fled to Pocasset, hoping to find allies in their uprising.

King Philip's War

When Philip and the others arrived, they found the Pocasset Indians eager to join their cause. While the warriors were preparing for battle, the English army was also making preparations. About two hundred white soldiers confronted members of the Narraganset tribe, preventing them from entering the war on the side of the Wampanoag. Meanwhile, native forces led by Philip began to strike at white villages.

The Wampanoag attacked Middleborough, the small settlement where Sassamon's body had been found months earlier. Next to fall under attack were settlements at Rehoboth and Taunton. At Dartmouth, settlers were killed and their bodies were mutilated. More than twenty-five houses were burned to the ground. Philip was not among the raiders, however. He spent most of his time hiding in the Pocasset swamp, planning and coordinating the violence that was consuming the region.

The Wampanoag and their allies set fire to a colonial settlement in Massachusetts during King Philip's War.

On August 1 a combined force of colonists and about forty Mohegan Indian scouts were met by a group of Wampanoag near Providence, Rhode Island. The colonists killed about fifty Wampanoag warriors. Philip and his tribesmen fled north to recruit more allies.

Philip's years of diplomacy had borne fruit in the north. When the Nipmuck tribe heard of the early successes experienced by Philip's warriors, it attacked several colonial establishments, later ambushing a party of whites sent from Boston to ask for peace. The tribe welcomed Philip and joined him in attacking settlements in the Connecticut River valley.

As the panic of the settlers intensified, the English unwittingly aided Philip's cause by attacking any and all Native Americans—even those sympathetic to the British cause. Troops burned villages as well as supplies belonging to friendly Pocumtook, Nonatook, Squakheag, and Nashaway tribes—all tribes that had long lived in peace with the colonists—so these tribes rose in vengeance and joined with Philip's warriors.

As 1675 drew to a close, colonial soldiers assaulted a Narraganset village on a snowy December day. The soldiers set fire to five hundred dwellings in the village, and the flames were whipped to a fury by the icy north wind. More than six hundred men, women, and children were "terribly barbecued,"[22] according to Puritan cleric Cotton Mather. Afterwards, soldiers who were horrified by the scene "seriously inquired whether burning their enemies alive could be consistent with humanity and the benevolent principles of the gospel."[23]

More than two thousand Narraganset Indians escaped, however, and after the horrific attack they, too, were eager to join forces with Philip and his other allies.

The Tide of War Turns

In February 1676, with the help of his former enemies, Philip's forces launched a new wave of attacks in central Massachusetts. Philip's orders were simple: Burn all the buildings and kill all the settlers until no whites are left. Before long southern New England was lit up with flames. On February 9 the Native Americans burned Lancaster, killing fifty whites. On February 20 they assaulted Medfield, less than twenty miles from Boston. As the buildings burned, the Native Americans left a written note nearby: "Know by this paper, that the Indians that thou hast provoked to wrath and anger, will war this twenty one years if you will."[24]

In May, Philip's warriors daringly burned sixteen homesteads within five miles of Plymouth. By the end of the spring, the grand sachem's men had struck fifty-two of the ninety settlements in the region, destroying twelve, completely damaging many others, and killing more than six hundred whites. Victory for the Native Americans seemed at hand.

The tribes, however, had no experience sustaining a long military campaign. A year of fighting had consumed almost all of the Native Americans' food. Some warriors were forced to quit fighting and return to their gardens for the summer season. Others left for hunting grounds to feed their starving families.

On the other side, the Indian victories only increased the English resolve to eradicate the Native Americans once and for all. The British put more soldiers into the field, who were joined by remaining allies from the Pequot, Mohegan, and Niantic tribes. Facing a foe who used Indian fighting tactics, Philip's warriors began to fall victim to the same types of ambushes and surprise attacks that they had employed against the settlers.

A combined English and Indian fighting force began to turn the tide of war. The Narraganset suffered a series of defeats, and isolated bands of the Nipmuck tribe began to surrender. Even King Philip's own people started to turn against him.

In the early summer of 1676, the Saconet band of the Wampanoag asked the English for peace. In hopes of gaining merciful treatment, Saconet war chiefs offered to take the English to Philip's camp. On July 30, 1676, a mixed company of Indians and soldiers ambushed King Philip and his followers in a swamp near Bridgewater. Philip escaped, but 173 of his people, including his uncle, were killed. Philip's wife and nine-year-old son were taken as prisoners and were sold as slaves to English planters in the West Indies. "My heart breaks," Philip reportedly cried out after the battle; "now I am ready to die."[25]

With his fighting alliance in tatters and his own tribe shrinking, Philip went back to his ancestral village to die. His hatred of the British still raged, however. When a warrior suggested he make peace with the whites, Philip had the man killed. In revenge, the man's brother defected to the English and offered them the head of the Wampanoag grand sachem.

As dawn broke on August 12, 1676, a volley of musket fire crashed into King Philip's camp. The sachem raced for the safety of a nearby swamp, but waiting in his line of flight was a colonist named Cook and a Pocasset Indian called Alderman. Cook pulled the trigger of his gun, but it misfired. He ordered Alderman to fire. Alderman's bullet pierced King Philip's heart.

Philip's head and hands were cut off, and his body was quartered. His body parts were strewn in the nearby woods, but his head was put on display at the Plymouth settlement for at least twenty years. Alderman kept one of Philip's hands and would display the grisly souvenir to anyone willing to pay a small price. Increase Mather, Cotton's son, kept Philip's lower jaw as a trophy.

The Aftermath

When King Philip fell in the summer of 1676, so too did the last hope of preserving the ancestral homes of New England's Native Americans. About twenty-five hundred colonists died in the battles that would later be called King Philip's War. Although the settlers won, the death toll seriously hampered New England's expansion for more than a century and heightened hatred of Native Americans. For years after the war, "Indian hunting" was a popular sport among

King Philip is shot through the heart while fleeing an ambush.

whites, who stalked Native Americans like animals.

The death toll among Native Americans in King Philip's War was far greater than that suffered by whites. Six thousand were wounded, killed, or sold into slavery to cover the cost of the war, and almost all the leaders were killed in battle or executed when captured. All Native American lands were confiscated in 1686, and all Indians were barred from hunting in the areas. Twenty years after the war's end, a Frenchman visiting the area reported: "There is Nothing to fear from the Savages. . . . The last Wars they had with the English . . . have reduced them to a small Number, and consequently they are incapable of defending themselves."[26]

When faced with the destruction of his people by the colonists, Philip bravely refused to give in. But his determined resistance to English demands led to a destructive war. Not only was King Philip killed, but his people were virtually destroyed. The unique knowledge and culture of the Wampanoag tribespeople were extinct—their spirits forever vanquished from the deep green forests of New England.

Chapter 3

Chief Pontiac

King Philip's War was the last such resistance to white settlers for nearly a century. It was not until the 1760s that a new battle would be led by an Ottawa chief named Pontiac in a region many hundreds of miles from New England. Although it was a different time and place, Pontiac's reasons for war were the same as King Philip's: to stop English occupation of Native American land.

Pontiac was born sometime in the 1720s. Historians differ on his place of birth; some say it was on the Maumee River in present-day Ohio, others say he was born on the north bank of the Detroit River near present-day Detroit, Michigan. The Ottawa tribe kept no written records, and since its members migrated from season to season, Pontiac's place of birth may have depended on the season of the year and whether his tribe was hunting in Michigan or farming in Ohio.

Ottawa chief Pontiac rallied his tribe against white encroachment in the Great Lakes region.

Pontiac's father was believed to be a subchief from the Ottawa tribe, and his mother was an Ojibwa from the Lake Superior region. In his native tongue, Pontiac's name meant "Stopping It" and was spelled Bwondiac or Obwandiyag. Following Ottawa custom, Pontiac's name was given to him at a special naming ceremony when he was a few months old. Later in the ceremony his ears and nose were pierced with sharpened bones. Members of the Ottawa tribe believed that the piercings would protect him from evil.

Little is known about Pontiac's early life. He probably grew up like other Ottawa boys playing war games, hunting, and fishing during the day and sleeping at night with his family in the community longhouse. Like other boys, he undoubtedly participated in his village's feasts and religious ceremonies.

When Pontiac reached adolescence he accompanied his father into battle against enemy tribes. As a tall, powerfully built young man, Pontiac was an honored warrior while still a teenager. Like other young warriors, the Ottawa boy fought hand-to-hand combat and helped torture defeated enemies. After a battle was won, young men like Pontiac looked on as peace treaties were negotiated by elders and solemnized by the ritual smoking of a peace pipe filled with tobacco and herbs.

As Pontiac grew older, he married two wives, as was the custom of many Native American tribes. Later he became the father of several children.

The French Demand for Furs

The territory where Pontiac and his people made their homes had long been claimed by the king of France. Decades before the Puritans clashed with the Wampanoag in New England, French explorers, traders, and missionaries had traveled far into the heart of the Great Lakes region. The Europeans established a string of trading posts and forts along the St. Lawrence River; Lakes Ontario, Erie, and Huron; and in the woods and valleys east of the Appalachian Mountains in present-day Pennsylvania and Ohio. By the time Pontiac was born, Americans referred to the area of the Great Lakes region as the Northwest Territory. The French called it Pay d'en haut—meaning "the Upper Country."

The hearty French traders, priests, and trappers who traveled through the Upper Country were not interested in taking Native American lands. Few in number, they only wanted small plots of land to build their forts and trading posts. Farming held little attraction for these Europeans, whose main interest was "brown gold"—pelts from beavers, marten, foxes, otters, panthers, bears, deer, and other furbearing animals.

Fur trappers could earn a good living. From the seventeenth century until the middle of the nineteenth century, no proper European gentleman would appear in public without a beaver hat perched on his head. European men and women also valued clothing with fur collars, cuffs, and other decorations. Fur trappers and hatters could barely keep up with the demand. In 1760 alone, one trading company exported enough beaver pelts to England to make 576,000 hats.

To obtain their pelts, the French organized the tribes of the Great Lakes region into a vast trading system that sent fleets of fur-laden ships down the St. Lawrence to the small frontier settlements of Montreal and Quebec. Furs were then loaded onto ships bound for European ports.

Most Native Americans found easy friendship with the French, who often married Native American women and made few territorial demands from the tribes. The guns, gunpowder, cooking utensils, beads, cloth, and other trade items brought by the French enhanced the cooperation between the two cultures.

The Ottawa Traders

Pontiac's Ottawa tribe was one of the many allies of the French. The tribe first encountered the Europeans in 1615 along Georgian Bay on the north shore of Lake Huron. The Native Americans lived in dozens of separate villages in the region. Although they hunted, farmed, and fished like other tribes, members of the Ottawa tribe were best known as traders. In fact, in the Algonquian language, *Ottawa* means "to buy and sell." Pontiac's forefathers routinely traveled hundreds of miles on foot or by canoe, visiting tribe after tribe with tobacco, cornmeal, furs, roots, herbs, precious metals, shells, and other items for sale or trade.

Members of the Ottawa tribe, well known as traders, enjoyed friendly relations with French merchants.

When white people arrived, they unknowingly upset this balance of trade. Their insatiable demand for furs and their imported guns and other items often led to violent competition between tribes. In addition, beavers were being trapped into extinction in the region. Tribes that traded with the French were increasingly forced to trap beaver on hunting grounds claimed by rival tribes, further increasing hostilities.

As Native Americans began to rely on European trade goods, they quickly lost the ability to make those items from stone, wood, and animal bones and skins as they had for centuries. As guns replaced traditional hunting methods, the skills needed for hunting with bows and arrows were almost completely forgotten. According to *The Mighty Chieftains,* trade with the Europeans became mandatory for survival:

> The European influence on [Ottawa] society was pervasive. Steel and iron hatchets and knives supplanted stone tools; brass kettles had replaced clay pots and tightly woven baskets for cooking; clothes were made of wool and cotton fabrics instead of animal skins; and most important, warriors came to rely almost entirely on guns for hunting and fighting.[27]

The Ottawa tribe was caught in the competition between tribes. In the 1640s the French were allied with the Huron tribe, or Wyandot, as they called themselves. The British—who were rivals of the French—backed the tribes of the Iroquois Nation living in present-day New York. The Iroquois attacked the Huron tribe, virtually destroying it. The Ottawa moved into this void to trade with the French, but the Iroquois attacked it, too. The Ottawa tribe was forced from its ancestral lands, and it moved as far west as the Mississippi River in 1657.

By strengthening its alliances with other tribes, the Ottawa soon returned to trade with the French. By 1680 Pontiac's people provided two-thirds of all beaver pelts sold to the French. This made them strong and wealthy and helped them create a trade network from the Mississippi River, reaching north to the Great Lakes and southeast to the Appalachian Mountains.

The French Abandon the Ottawa Tribe

Although the French dominated the fur business, British trappers began appearing in Ottawa country sometime around 1740. These trappers offered trade goods that were of superior quality and asked for fewer pelts in return. The Ottawa tribe remained allied to the French, however, although some other tribes switched allegiance to the British. In the 1750s British and French rivalries burst into full-scale war; these battles are known as the French and Indian War. The Ottawa and most of the western tribes sided with the French and helped France win several important victories. The outcome of the war, however, was decided not on the Indian frontier but by European-type battles fought with uniformed soldiers, large cannons, and ships in Quebec, Montreal, and elsewhere. The French were defeated and withdrew their forces from Canada in 1760.

Pontiac and his people were stunned, but the full consequences of the defeat were yet to unfold. Pontiac was present when British troops arrived in Fort Detroit in November 1760 to hold conferences with the Ottawa, Huron, and Potawatomi tribes. British Indian agent George Croghan told the assembled leaders that the British would continue benevolent French policies in the area. What Croghan failed to mention was that Great Britain had claimed the entire area and that all residents of the territory—Indian and white—were now subjects of the English Crown.

The commander in chief of the new British holdings, Sir Jeffrey Amherst, had won fame on the battlefields of Europe and had no affection for Native Americans, whom he considered barbarians. According to Amherst, "The only true method of treating the savages is to keep them in proper subjugation and punish, without exception, the transgressors." [28]

Amherst sent Major Robert Rogers to take possession of the new English holdings. On the way, Rogers met Pontiac. Rogers wrote about their meeting in his journal, which is quoted in *Pontiac and the Indian Uprising*:

> The Indians on the lakes . . . are formed into sort of an empire, and the Emperor is elected from the eldest tribe, which is the Ottawas. . . . Ponteack is their present King or Emperor, who has certainly the largest empire and greatest authority of any Indian Chief. . . . He puts on an air of majesty and princely grandeur, and is greatly honored and revered by his subjects.
>
> At first salutation when we met, he demanded my business into his country, and how it happened that I dared to enter it without his leave? When I informed him that . . . I came . . . to remove the French out of this country [he] gave me no other answer. [29]

The French and Indian War

The French and Indian War was fought between England's colonies in North America and the French in America and Canada. Other battles involved Spain in Florida. The series of conflicts lasted seventy-four years, from 1689 to 1763, when the French were defeated. Native Americans fought on one side or the other, often with disastrous results for the tribes.

The long, bloody war caused great suffering for everyone involved. Frontier settlers were often caught in the middle of enemy raids, sometimes losing their homes and their lives. Enemy Native Americans were hunted like animals and scalped so the killers could claim a cash bounty offered by the colonial government.

England won through sheer numbers. In 1689 the area known as New France had only about 12,000 inhabitants while the English colonists numbered over 200,000. By the end of the war in 1763 the population of New France was about 60,000, but the British colonies had grown to nearly 1.6 million people, not including Native Americans.

The Treaty of Paris, signed in 1763, awarded Great Britain all of North America east of the Mississippi River, including Canada and Florida. This would begin a new series of conflicts between the British and the Native American tribes who had inhabited the land for millennia.

Native Americans are brutally slaughtered by English colonists during the French and Indian War.

Signifying his desire to live in peace with the English, Pontiac shares a peace pipe with Major Robert Rogers.

Pontiac took the news impassively, turned, and rode away. The next day he returned with his braves. With great ceremony Pontiac said he would live peacefully beside his new neighbors if they treated him "with the respect and honor due to a King or Emperor." [30] If the British mistreated his people, however, Pontiac threatened to cut off their route to the interior of the country.

Relations between the British and Ottawa soured almost immediately. Amherst did not understand the importance of gift giving among the Native Americans, and he ordered his commanders to stop giving arms, ammunition, and clothing to the tribes, as the French had done. Any trading with the Native Americans was to be conducted only at official trading posts.

The denial of guns and emergency food rations caused immediate distress in some villages. Many tribes lived far from trading posts and resented having to travel long distances to sell pelts and receive trade goods. Pontiac began to speak out against the British.

Pontiac Spreads a Prophet's Message

Pontiac had exhibited great skill and bravery during the French and Indian War. Now his talent for battle was replaced by his gift for oratory. The great leader could hold audiences at rapt attention for hours. Even the whites were impressed by Pontiac's speaking ability, although many were frightened by his appearance. Like other Ottawa warriors, Pontiac was heavily tattooed. He wore his hair short, and it stood upright in front in a style known as a warlock. Pontiac's face was painted and he decorated himself with silver bracelets, a stone through his pierced nose, and beaded earrings.

Wherever Pontiac went, he accused the British of selling shoddy goods and cheating his people. Rumors spread among native tribes that France was about to fight another war with Great

Britain to retake Canada. For several years Pontiac made the most of this rumor as he traveled from village to village convincing other tribes to unite under his command. Pontiac's audiences grew ever larger as he spread his message of resistance.

Meanwhile, a holy man named Neolin from the Delaware tribe began preaching his own message. The fortunes of the Native Americans were declining, Neolin said, because of the corrupting influence of whites and the sinfulness of Native Americans. Neolin said that addiction to rum and the failure to observe proper rituals angered the guardian spirits. To fight back, Native Americans should commit themselves to sobriety, self-sufficiency, and intertribal peace.

Pontiac took Neolin's message to other tribes in the region. The great chief's words were reprinted in David Horowitz's *The First Frontier*. In Pontiac's account, the Great Spirit told him,

> I am the Maker of heaven and earth, the trees, lakes, rivers, and all things else. I am the Maker of mankind. . . . The land on which you live I have made for you, and not for others. Why do you suffer the white men to dwell among you? My children, you have forgotten the customs and traditions of your forefathers. Why do you not clothe yourselves in skins, as they did, and use the bows and arrows, and the stone-pointed lances, which they used. You have bought guns, knives, kettles, and blankets, from the white men, until you can no longer do without them; and what is worse, you have drunk the poison firewater, which turns you into fools. Fling all these things away; live as your wise forefathers lived before you. And as for these English—these dogs dressed in red, who have come to rob you of your hunting-grounds, and drive away the game— you must lift the hatchet against them. Wipe them from the face of the earth.[31]

Pontiac's message spread through the Ohio Valley and the northern Great Lakes region like wildfire. And more good news reached Pontiac: The Seneca in New York, who had long been friends with the British, were ready to fight their former allies as white settlers made more demands for Native American land.

Pontiac received many other pledges of support for his proposed war against the British. French traders assured him that help would be coming from Louisiana, a territory still owned by France. Pontiac drew up battle plans and sent runners to other tribes to urge them to join his war. Belts, called wampum, whose

Chief Pontiac meets with tribesmen to spread holy man Neolin's prophetic message and call for unity among the tribes.

beads were arranged in a pattern calling for war, were circulated among the Delaware, Ottawa, and Potawatomi tribes. Within months the Mohawk, Shawnee, and Oneida in present-day New York were ready to join against the British.

The plans for rebellion were set when twenty thousand Native Americans joined Pontiac's secret war council at the end of April 1763. A week later, Pontiac planned to mount his first attack.

Attacking Fort Detroit

On May 7, 1763, Pontiac and three hundred warriors bluffed their way into Fort Detroit under the guise of performing a ceremonial dance for the soldiers. Once inside, they planned to take over the fort with the sawed-off muskets, knives, and hatchets they had hidden under their blankets. The fort's commander, Major Henry Gladwin, however, had been warned of the attack by spies, and Pontiac's warriors were faced with well-armed British soldiers. Fearing disaster, Pontiac called off the assault and his warriors timidly left the fort.

Pontiac was severely criticized by his warriors when he backed down. To gain back his good standing and take advantage of his ready warriors, Pontiac called for an immediate war. According to *The Mighty Chieftains,*

> Having failed to take the fort by stealth, he would now besiege it, killing all Englishmen found outside the walls and starving those within. In the meantime, raiding parties would

fan out to attack other British forts while runners carried war belts to enlist the help of their neighboring tribes.[32]

Two days after the failed incident at Fort Detroit, Pontiac's warriors attacked and scalped three white settlers who lived in clear view of the fort. As soldiers watched helplessly, warriors then raced to their canoes and paddled out to a nearby island to kill and scalp five more people. In Pontiac's village, 460 warriors prepared to assail Fort Detroit.

The next day frightened soldiers cowered in the fort as stories of Native American exploits reached them. Rumor had it that two English officers had been attacked near Lake St. Clair, and the Native Americans had boiled and eaten one man and tanned his skin for use as a tobacco pouch. Meanwhile, a large war party of Ottawa, Potawatomi, and Ojibwa warriors crept up to the fort. While concealed behind fallen trees and abandoned buildings, they began a six-hour barrage of musket fire aimed at the English soldiers within. The English soldiers in Fort Detroit held back the Indian assault for weeks. Other forts were less successful.

A Round of Easy Victories

One week after the attack on Fort Detroit, a band of Ottawa and Huron warriors captured Fort Sandusky, located to the east on the shores of Lake Erie. By the end of May, the Potawatomi had taken Fort Joseph near present-day South Bend, Indiana, after killing or capturing all of its defenders. Miami and Ottawa warriors subdued Fort Miami in Ohio.

With a string of successes, Pontiac received more good news. More eastern and western tribes had responded to his call and were rising up against the British, seizing forts, and wiping out settlers and settlements. From the Ojibwa in the north to the Delaware in western Pennsylvania, tribes laid waste to villages and forts, putting homesteads to the torch and killing inhabitants by burning them alive.

Pontiac's own braves had attacked a British supply fleet thirty miles southeast of Detroit. Less then half of the ninety-six-man detachment had escaped; later, victorious Indians sailed eight huge canoes filled with provisions and prisoners past the British forts to their own villages.

Less than two months after the first shots were fired at Fort Detroit, Pontiac and his allies had assaulted thirteen British forts and captured nine. Two of the remaining four were under siege. The Native Americans had killed at least two thousand people. White survivors escaped east across the Appalachian Mountains with their families. Not since the days of King Philip had there been such a large organized uprising on the American frontier.

The British Strike Back

By the summer of 1763 Pontiac's forces were at a high point in their struggle to rid their territory of white people. At this time, however, the war chief received some bad tidings. The British and French had signed a peace treaty officially concluding the French and Indian War. Pontiac, still hoping for reinforcement from French troops, discounted the news, but without French support, a number of Pontiac's allies began to question the wisdom of continuing the war since the British were not about to surrender.

On July 28, under a heavy cover of fog, 260 British soldiers sneaked past Native Americans guarding the Detroit River. They planned to rest for two days, then attack Pontiac's village under cover of darkness. Anticipating their movements, Pontiac set up an ambush and sprung a trap on the unsuspecting British, who were silhouetted by a bright moon. Ottawa warriors fired on the soldiers for more than an hour, killing twenty of them and wounding thirty-four. Survivors fled to Fort Detroit, more than doubling the number of soldiers in the garrison.

The British named the site of the ambush Bloody Run. The news of the Bloody Run massacre so angered Sir Jeffrey Amherst that he offered a reward of one hundred pounds to any man who could kill Pontiac. He also proposed spreading smallpox among the Indians by giving them germ-laden blankets.

During Pontiac's war with the British, Ottawa warriors ambush English soldiers at what was later known as Bloody Run.

Eighteenth-Century Biological Warfare

The British suffered a string of embarrassing and deadly losses to Pontiac's forces, but they had more than guns and cannons in their arsenal. Following a massacre of British soldiers at Bloody Run, British general Sir Jeffrey Amherst sent a letter to his field commander, Henry Bouquet, telling the commander to infect the Native Americans with small-pox. The scheme is detailed in The First Frontier *by David Horowitz.*

"[Amherst wrote]: 'Could it not be contrived to send the *Small Pox* among these disaffected tribes of Indians? We must on this occasion use every stratagem in our power to reduce them. . . .'

Bouquet, who was preparing to lead a force . . . agreed. He would try, he said, to infect the Indians with some contaminated blankets, and he expressed the wish that they could use English dogs to hunt them, 'as it is a pity to expose good men against them.'

General Amherst approved of the scheme: 'You will do well to try to inoculate the Indians by means of blankets, as well as to try every other method that can serve to extirpate [wipe out] this execrable race.' "

Despite Pontiac's best efforts to bring it down, Fort Detroit was still held by the British. Although 870 warriors surrounded the fort, supplies continued to trickle in through the siege lines. As the cold winds of September began to blow, Fort Detroit was stronger than ever. If the warriors and their families were to survive the winter, they needed to stop fighting and begin the autumn hunt. In addition, hundreds of Native Americans from a half dozen tribes were dying from Amherst's smallpox-laden blankets. With the fighting forces in disarray, large bands of Huron, Potawatomi, and Ottawa Indians let it be known to the British that they no longer had the will to fight.

By October warriors were drifting off to their hunting grounds, and Pontiac's last hopes of help from the French were dashed. A commander at a French outpost on the Mississippi River wrote to the chief, informing him that the kings of France and England had made peace. The commander urged Pontiac to do the same. Under the peace agreement, the French had sworn to side with Great Britain in battle. To attack England was to attack France, and Pontiac could not expect to fight both countries at once.

It was difficult for Pontiac to believe that he had been abandoned by the French, whom he had aided in the French and Indian War. Worse, Pontiac had been abandoned by many of his own people. The great chief realized that to continue fighting would only cause great harm. His rebellion was threatening the trade economy of the Ottawa and would now bring the wrath of both the British and the French. As if to deliver a final blow, when the French messenger left, the season's first snowfall blanketed the ground.

On October 31, 1763, Pontiac sent a letter of surrender to Major Gladwin. It was transcribed for him by a French sympathizer and was reprinted in *Pontiac and the Indian Uprising*. Pontiac's letter read:

> My Brother: The word which my father [the French commander] has sent me to make peace I have accepted; all my young men have buried their hatchets. I think you will forget the bad things which have taken place for time past. Likewise I shall forget what you may have done to me, in order to think of nothing but good. I, the [Ojibwa], the Hurons, we are ready to go speak with you when you ask us. Give us an answer. I am sending this resolution to you in order that you may see it. If you are as kind as I, you will make me a reply. I wish you a good day. "Pontiac" [33]

Gladwin refused to meet with Pontiac. Instead, he replied that Amherst would negotiate peace. Then Gladwin wrote a note to Amherst coolly describing the situation of Pontiac and his allies.

> They have lost between 80 and 90 of their best warriors; but if your Excellency still intends to punish them further for their barbarities, it may be easily done without any expense to the Crown by permitting a free sale of rum, which will destroy them more effectually than fire and sword. But on the contrary, if you intend to accommodate matters in the spring . . . by that time the savages will be sufficiently reduced for want of powder. . . . No advantages can be gained by prosecuting the war, owing to the difficulty of catching them; add to this the expense of such a war which, if continued, the entire ruin of our peltry trade must follow, and the loss of a prodigious consumption of our merchandises. [34]

Dying Alone

Gladwin's letter never received an answer from Amherst because Amherst had been replaced by Major General Thomas Gage. Gage believed fighting western Indians was a waste of time and told his officers in the field to seek peace. By mid-November, however, Pontiac had received no answer from any British authorities, so he left Detroit with a band of loyal followers to live along the Maumee River near present-day Waterville, Ohio.

Pontiac spent a cold winter with bitter memories. In the spring he went to live among the Illinois tribe. He urged his followers to renew the fight. His deputies traveled far south down the Mississippi River to enlist the southern tribes, but their mission was a failure. By August 1764 the Seneca, Menominee, Sauk, and Fox had signed peace treaties with the British.

In the summer of 1765, Pontiac attended a British peace conference held outside the gates of Fort Detroit. The Ottawa chief told George Croghan that the surrounding lands belonged to the Native Americans. Croghan countered that Indian nations were not recognized by international law and had no rights to the land. The British gave Pontiac presents but refused to honor any land claims. Pontiac conceded and solemnly signed a peace treaty.

The British were impressed with the chief's intelligence and decided not to punish him for the war. But the British admiration for Pontiac caused him to lose respect among the Ottawa, and the fallen leader soon became an outcast among his own people. He found little support from young warriors, who refused to accept him as their leader. Humiliated, Pontiac went to live with relatives in the Illinois tribe in 1768.

Pontiac found no more support among the Illinois. Two years earlier he had stabbed an Illinois chief in a quarrel, and other tribespeople treated him coldly. The victim's relatives were bent on revenge. On

A fanciful re-creation portrays an ostracized Pontiac moments before he is clubbed to death by an Illinois warrior.

April 20, 1769, Pontiac entered a French trading store on the banks of the Mississippi River. A warrior struck Pontiac from behind with a club, then stabbed him. The Ottawa chief fell over and died. And although five years earlier he had led thousands of men in a brave war against the British, the Ottawa grand chief had not a single follower to avenge his death.

CHAPTER 4

Geronimo

The failure of Pontiac and his allies to drive the British from the Northwest Territory was only the beginning of Native American losses in the area. Americans won independence from the British in 1781, and the victors continued the British policy of eradicating Native Americans.

In the 1830s, in the same areas where Pontiac's rebellion was fought, Native Americans united behind a chief of the Sauk tribe named Black Hawk. In 1835, after losing several battles in what was known as Black Hawk's War, the Sauk, Fox, Ojibwa, Menominee, Iowa, Huron, Ottawa, and Potawatomi tribes signed treaties ceding their ancestral lands to the U.S. government. By the 1840s the tribes were confined on tiny reservations in barren areas of Oklahoma and elsewhere, and they were forced to live with poverty and starvation.

Legendary Apache chief Geronimo displays his characteristic scowl and fierce demeanor in an 1887 photograph.

Geronimo was an Apache chief who would continue the Native American resistance to white settlement far to the southwest in Arizona. He was born in 1829 in the forbidding mountains clustered around the Gila River in Arizona, then part of Mexico. The problems Black Hawk and his people were facing could not have seemed farther away. At that time there were no railroads and few wagon tracks through southeastern Arizona and western New Mexico, where the Apache resided. But the problems the Apache were about to face in the southwest were the same difficulties

54

facing their Midwestern cousins: They lived in a land that was soon to be claimed by the United States of America. They could either surrender to U.S. demands or die fighting.

One Who Yawns

Geronimo was born near the present-day town of Clifton, Arizona. The sleepy baby was given the name Goyahkla (sometimes spelled Goyathlay), meaning "One Who Yawns," although this could not have been a less appropriate name for the energetic adult Geronimo would become. Goyahkla's family belonged to the Bedonkohé band of Chiricahua Apache, who lived on the Mogollon Range near the headwaters of the Gila River. His father was called Taklishim, "the Gray One," and his mother, although a full-blooded Apache, had the Spanish name of Juana.

Goyahkla often assisted his mother and father farm small plots of corn, beans, and pumpkins. He also helped make *tizwin*, a beer of fermented crushed corn. Goyahkla also accompanied his family on trips to gather wild plants and herbs.

One of the wild plants harvested by the Apache was tobacco, which men and women smoked rolled like cigarettes in oak leaf wrappers. Boys were not allowed to smoke until they had hunted alone and killed large game such as wolves and bears. Unmarried

Tizwin

The great majority of Native Americans did not drink alcohol before Europeans sold it to them. No tribes actually made alcoholic beverages except the Apache, who brewed a type of beer from corn called tizwin. *The details of the* tizwin *ritual are related by Angie Debo in* Geronimo: The Man, His Time, His Place.

"[*Tizwin* was] prepared by the women with the help of the children. They may have learned the technique from the Indians in Old Mexico or from the Spanish-speaking Mexicans. First they soaked the corn overnight in water. They dug a long trench and lined it with grass, placed the soaked corn in the trench, and covered it with another layer of grass. Sometimes they covered the whole with earth or with a blanket. After sprinkling the corn with water morning and evening for ten days, during which it sprouted, they took it out, ground it with their grinding stones . . . and then boiled it for four or five hours. Finally, they strained off the liquid and set it aside. After about twenty-four hours, when it stopped bubbling, it was ready to drink."

women were not prohibited from smoking but were considered immodest if they did so. Nearly all older women smoked.

The Apache depended on herbs for healing, as Geronimo writes in his 1906 autobiography:

> The Indians knew what herbs to use for medicine, how to prepare them, and how to give the medicine. This they had been taught by Usen [the Supreme Being] from the beginning. . . .
>
> In gathering the herbs, in preparing them, and administering the medicine, as much faith was held in prayer as in the actual effect of the medicine. Usually about eight persons worked together in making medicine and there were forms of prayer and incantations to attend each stage of the process.[35]

When Goyahkla was about ten, he joined the Apache men in hunting expeditions. As he later wrote,

> Out on the prairies, which ran up to our mountain homes, wandered herds of deer, antelope, elk, and buffalo to be slaughtered when we needed them.
>
> Usually we hunted buffalo on horseback, killing them with arrows and spears. Their skins were used to make tepees and bedding; their flesh, to eat.[36]

Geronimo also hunted bears and mountain lions as well as rabbits, wild turkeys, and other game. Eagles were hunted for their feathers, which had great value since it took enormous skill to catch an eagle.

Although Geronimo's hunting expeditions helped him learn skills also used in battle, the young Apache grew up in a time of peace for his people. As he later wrote in his autobiography, "During my [childhood], we never saw a missionary or priest. We never saw a white man. Thus quietly lived the Bedonkohé Apaches."[37]

Learning from the Nednhi

Although his tribe lived in peace, Goyahkla, like all Apache males, trained for warfare from boyhood. As a teenager, he learned to travel through his sacred homeland by memorizing every rock and crevice of the rough terrain. In the mornings Goyahkla would plunge into the nearest creek with his companions, even if the boys had to break the ice to do so.

Goyahkla's tribe was closely related to the Nednhi Apache who drew their existence from repeatedly raiding Mexican settlements and trading the goods they stole. When a band of Nednhi came to visit the Bedonkohé, a teen named Juh, or "Whoa," the son of a Nednhi chief, befriended Goyahkla. Juh taught Goyahkla the warlike ways of the Nednhi, and the two teenagers soon came to regard each other as brothers.

When Goyahkla was a teenager, his father died. The Gray One was buried in a mountain cave in his finest ceremonial clothes; his face was painted, and he was wrapped in a beautiful blanket. In accordance with Apache tradition, the Gray One's horse was shot, his belongings were destroyed, and his name was never spoken again. As Geronimo later wrote: "Wrapped in splendor he lies in seclusion, and the winds in the pines sing a low requiem over the dead warrior." [38]

After his father's death, Goyahkla assumed the care of his mother. In their grief and loneliness, Goyahkla and Juana decided to visit Juh and other relatives among the Nednhi in the Sierra Madre mountains. It was a perilous journey through parched lands. Even when they reached the homelands of the Nednhi, it was difficult for Goyahkla to find the tribe because its members expertly concealed their trails and left little evidence of their existence.

Living among the Nednhi, Goyahkla developed his skills as a warrior. According to Geronimo biographer Angie Debo,

> First the youth was taught the rules of survival. Have the women [prepare] enough meat and fat for a week's food, and take along a supply of water. Cross open flats by night, and reach a mountain and hide in the brush by day. Locate water holes by climbing to a high place and looking for green spots; but do not go to them by day, only at night. . . . If you become lost and want to call for help, make a fire and send up a smoke signal. . . .
>
> After the youth mastered these techniques, he might volunteer to join a hostile expedition. As an apprentice warrior . . . he . . . [was] required to perform all the work about camp—caring for the horses, getting water and wood, doing the cooking, serving on guard duty. If he showed courage and dependability on four expeditions (Apaches . . . regarded four as a sacred number) he was accepted as a warrior, a man among men. [39]

Goyahkla was admitted to the council of warriors at the age of seventeen and was soon accompanying Juh and the Nednhi on raids of Mexican pack trains, killing the men and stealing their horses, food, and freight.

Apache warriors often formed raiding parties for looting enemy villages and Mexican pack trains.

As a reward for his efforts, Goyahkla was permitted to marry Alope, the young Nednhi woman he had been courting. Geronimo later recounted:

> Perhaps the greatest joy for me was that I could marry the fair Alope, daughter of No-po-so. She was a slender, delicate girl, but we had been lovers for a long time. . . . I went to see her father concerning our marriage. Perhaps our love was not of interest to him; perhaps he wanted to keep Alope with him, for she was a dutiful daughter; at any rate he asked many ponies for her. I made no reply, but in a few days appeared before his wigwam with a herd of ponies and took with me Alope. This was all the marriage ceremony necessary in our tribe.
>
> Not far from my mother's tepee I had made for us a new home. The tepee was made of buffalo hides and in it were many bear robes, lion [cougar] hides, and other trophies of the chase, as well as my spears, bows, and arrows. Alope had made many decorations of beads and drawn work on buckskin, which she placed in our tepee. She also drew many pictures on the walls of our home. She was a good wife, but she was never strong. We followed the traditions of our fathers and were happy. Three children came to us— children that played, loitered, and worked as I had done.[40]

Hostility with Spain and Mexico

Although Geronimo grew up in a peaceful time, hostilities between Mexico and the Apache tribe dated back three centuries to the arrival of the Spanish conquistadors. When the Spaniards first arrived in Apache territory in 1540, they ensnared the Indians for sale as slaves. The Apache responded by mounting swift counterattacks against the Spanish army before vanishing into the mountains.

By 1630 the entire Apache culture was based on raiding settled Spanish communities. It was as much a way of life for them as was hunting or gathering berries. In Geronimo: The Man, His Time, His Place, *Angie Debo describes the Apache skills as raiders.*

"Long experience had taught them all the tricks of survival. They knew the location of every water hole and hidden canyon. Men, women, and children could travel with incredible speed and secrecy, striking their enemies here today, a hundred miles away on the other side of the mountain tomorrow. . . . Incidents growing out of this age-old pattern formed the immediate background of Geronimo's career as a warrior and raider."

Apache scalps such as this one brought rewards from the Mexican government.

The Spaniards responded to Apache raids with systematic attempts to exterminate the Indians. Mexico gained independence from Spain in 1821, but the new government did not give up its war against the Apache. In 1835 the Mexican government offered a one-hundred-peso reward (a considerable sum of money at that time) for every scalp of an Apache warrior. Women's scalps were worth fifty pesos, and children's were worth twenty-five pesos. This offer attracted roving bands of Americans who came to Mexican territory in order to take up the lucrative business of "scalp hunting."

The Apache in Mexico and the United States

In 1846 war broke out between the United States and Mexico. Goyahkla, who was living in the remote mountains, was not affected by the war. Although the Apache approved of the war, they did not approve of the peace that followed. In 1848 the Treaty of Guadalupe Hidalgo ended the Mexican War. As a result, the United States was awarded Texas, and Mexico ceded the territories that are now Arizona, New Mexico, and southern Colorado to the United States for $15 million.

An international border was drawn directly through the southern third of the Chiricahua Apache territory. In the treaty, the U.S. government pledged to prevent Indians in the region from crossing the border to conduct raids in Mexico. This provision quickly proved impossible to enforce across such a wide area of harsh country. The Apache, for their part, could not comprehend the American objection to raids that had been carried out for centuries.

In 1853 the Gadsden Purchase added more land from Mexico to the U.S. territories of New Mexico, Arizona, and California, finalizing their current borders. This brought all of the Chiricahua

lands under U.S. control. In 1855 the U.S. Army crushed resistance from the Jicarilla and Mescalero Apache tribes. This forced several of the Apache bands, including the Warm Springs, Mimbreño, and Mescalero, to relocate to a reservation on the Gila River in exchange for thirty-thousand-dollars' worth of food and supplies. The Mimbreño band acted peacefully for a time and farmed their American lands, but they later crossed the border to raid settlements in Mexico.

Goyahkla's Family Is Massacred

While other Apache bands had been moved to a reservation, Goyahkla still lived in his ancestral homeland. Although he was not yet thirty years old, Goyahkla had developed the fierce scowl seen in so many later photographs. He was a barrel-chested man, five feet eight inches tall, with a hawklike nose, jutting cheekbones, and a frowning slit of a mouth.

The frown grew deeper in the summer of 1858, after Goyahkla and his warriors rode into Mexico to trade and drink whiskey. Their band had set up a base camp outside of the town they called Kas-ki-yeh, later identified as Janos. Every day when they rode into Kas-ki-yeh, the Apache warriors left their camp under the protection of a small guard so that the women and children would not be disturbed in their absence. Then, as Geronimo later wrote,

> Late one afternoon when returning from town we were met by a few women and children who told us that Mexican troops . . . had attacked our camp, killed all our warriors of the guard, captured all our ponies, secured our arms, destroyed our supplies, and killed many of our women and children. . . . [When] all were counted, I found that my aged mother, my young wife, and my three small children were among the slain.[41]

A total of 130 people—mostly women and children—had been slaughtered. Later that night the Apache called a council and decided that since there were only eighty warriors left alive, and they were deep inside Mexican territory, that they would "start at once in perfect silence for our homes in Arizona, leaving the dead upon the field."[42]

On the long march home Goyahkla grieved in silence, feeling as though he had lost everything. When he returned to his village, according to custom, he burnt his family's and his mother's tepees and all of their possessions, including the children's toys. He later wrote, "I was never again contented in our quiet home. . . . I had vowed vengeance upon the Mexican troopers who had wronged me, and whenever I . . . saw anything to remind me of former happy days my heart would ache for revenge upon Mexico."[43]

Geronimo Finds Vengeance and a Name

At a war council following the massacre, Goyahkla spoke eloquently to the Chiricahua warriors, asking them to join him in battle against the Mexicans. Then he traveled south to the land of the Nednhi to enlist their help in retaliation for the massacre. In the summer of 1859, almost one year after the killing near Kas-ki-yeh, the warriors marched into Mexico to avenge the deaths of their people.

When they reached the town of Arispe, they were met by two companies of Mexican cavalry and two of infantry. Goyahkla recognized two soldiers, whom he believed had killed his family. He told one of his chieftains and was asked to lead the battle. According to Geronimo, "I was no chief and never had been, but because I had been more deeply wronged than others, this honor was conferred upon me, and I resolved to prove worthy of the trust."[44] After a long, bloody battle with many casualties on both sides, the Apache band finally declared victory. During the course of battle, the Mexican soldiers screamed "Geronimo!" (the Spanish equivalent of Jerome, their patron saint) whenever they attacked. Goyahkla also took up the cry of Geronimo, and so the Apache warrior found his adult name.

Geronimo (center) and his Chiricahua warriors pose for a photograph in the barren Arizona desert in 1886.

Other warriors were satisfied after the battle, but Geronimo still desired more revenge. He and two other warriors continued through Mexico attacking several towns and fighting off forces that greatly outnumbered them. When the other warriors were killed, Geronimo was finally chased back to his home in Arizona. Still, hatred for the Mexicans burned within him: "I never ceased to plan for their punishment."[45]

Geronimo soon married a new wife, who bore him two children; and a second wife, who also gave birth to a child. Not even the presence of Geronimo's new family lessened his hatred for the Mexicans. He raided villages and stole their horses to seek revenge. Between 1860 and 1868 Geronimo rode into Mexico with twenty-five or thirty warriors and fought vicious battles with Mexican soldiers. Geronimo writes about a typical battle, this one fought in 1861: "Bullets whistled in every direction and at close range to me. One inflicted a slight flesh wound on my side. I kept running, dodging, and fighting, until I got clear of my pursuers."[46] In addition to fighting soldiers, Geronimo's warriors successfully raided pack trains and villages, obtaining great quantities of food, mescal (liquor), horses, and cattle, which were taken back to the women and children at home.

Fighting the Americans

The battles of Geronimo and his warriors were not confined to Mexico. In 1868 the Apache tribe signed a peace treaty with the Americans. A year later, U.S. troops invited Apache leaders to a conference at Fort Bowie. The conference was a sham. Geronimo explains, "Just before noon, the Indians were shown into a tent and told that they would be given something to eat. When in the tent they were attacked by soldiers. Our chief . . . and several other warriors escaped; but most of the warriors were killed or captured."[47] The Apache retaliated by capturing a wagon train headed for the fort and killing several soldiers: "After this trouble all of the Indians agreed not to be friendly with the white men any more. . . . [This] treachery on the part of the soldiers had angered the Indians and revived memories of other wrongs, so that we never again trusted the United States troops."[48]

Geronimo joined with others to conduct raids on American soil. Because of these attacks, the United States had to stop using a stagecoach line through Apache Pass. The Apache rebels also cut off a vital supply road between Tucson and Tubac. By 1870 Indian attacks so preoccupied the army that U.S. general William Tecumseh Sherman said of the region, "We had one war with Mexico [to gain the territory] and we should have another to make her take [the region] back." [49]

But the Apache also understood that they would never drive the white settlers—whom they called "white eyes"—from the region. "We kill ten; another hundred come in their place," [50] one chief told his warriors.

Forced onto Reservations

Although Geronimo and his Apache warriors continued to raid in their traditional manner, they did not realize how large and powerful the United States was becoming. By the 1870s telegraph lines were winding their way across the American Southwest, allowing the army forts to communicate with other companies of soldiers across miles of desert. The American Civil War had ended in 1865, and hardened veterans of that war filled out the ranks of the U.S. Cavalry. Far away in Washington, D.C., President Ulysses S. Grant ordered General George Crook to Arizona to quell the Apache raids and force the Indians onto reservations.

This began more than fifteen years of struggle between Geronimo and the whites. The years were marked by the Apache moving onto reservations, corrupt government agencies failing to deliver promised food and rations, and the Apache escaping to raid, steal, and kill.

In 1875 the Bureau of Indian Affairs launched a disastrous policy of "concentration," attempting to settle all the various Apache bands (around forty-five

General George Crook ended Apache raids into Mexico and forced the tribe onto reservations.

hundred people) onto the San Carlos Reservation. Once there, the Apache were forced to obey rules that Crook had implemented with little knowledge of Apache culture or lifestyles. Every Indian was given a brass tag with a number on it, which was to be worn around the neck for identification purposes. The Apache were put to work digging a five-mile-long irrigation ditch using pointed sticks hardened in campfires rather than shovels. Since soldiers could not pronounce Apache names, the Indians were given more American-sounding names like "Joe" or "Bobbie."

Nearby, brackish water spawned millions of mosquitoes that spread malaria throughout the reservation. There was no grass and little game. Nearly all of the vegetation was cacti, and the summer temperatures reached over 110 degrees. The nomadic Apache could not grow crops on such arid lands, and the hated reservation picked up the nickname "Hell's Forty Acres."

Geronimo at San Carlos

In June 1876 authorities came for Geronimo's Chiricahua band to transport them to San Carlos. Geronimo fled to Mexico, where he resumed his raiding before returning to the United States again in March 1877. On April 21 Geronimo was arrested by eighty reservation police officers and was taken in chains to San Carlos.

San Carlos' authorities recognized Geronimo's influence over his people. They sought to win his cooperation by making him "captain" of the Warm Springs band of Apache at San Carlos. But Geronimo found life on the reservation intolerable and fled with his old friend Juh into the Sierra Madre mountains. Following a winter of hardship, Geronimo surrendered to authorities and, once again, returned to San Carlos.

For the next several years, Geronimo would live at San Carlos for a time, run away, and be forcibly returned again by the army. In 1881 Geronimo and seventy followers bolted from the reservation. After killing thirteen whites, they eluded fourteen hundred troops on a remarkable one thousand-mile trek along the border. They joined with other bands of Apache, crossed into Mexico, and fought Mexican soldiers. For two years the Apache rebels crossed back and forth across the border, terrorizing towns in Arizona and New Mexico. All the while they were pursued by General Crook and his soldiers. Finally, in January 1884, after his best warriors had been killed and one of his wives was captured, Geronimo returned to San Carlos. His stay lasted only briefly.

By May Geronimo was on the run again. This time Geronimo escaped with thirty-eight warriors and ninety-two women and children. Again they were pursued by Crook's troops, and again settlers were murdered along the way as well as many Native Americans. When Geronimo crossed into Mexico, he waged the same type of battles against Mexican soldiers. As Geronimo later recalled, "We attacked every Mexican we found, even if for no other reason than to kill. We believed they had asked the United States troops to come down to Mexico to fight us. . . . We were reckless of our lives, because we felt that every man's hand was against us."[51]

The Final Surrender

To quell disturbances at San Carlos, the Bureau of Indian Affairs had shipped many of Geronimo's Chiricahua tribespeople, including one of his wives, to a reservation at Fort Marion, Florida. Worried about his wife's safety, Geronimo surrendered for the last time on September 4, 1886, at Fort Bowie in southeastern Arizona. The Apache warrior said,

> We placed a large stone on the blanket before us. Our treaty was made by this stone, and it was to last until the stone should crumble into dust; so we made the treaty, and bound each other with an oath. I do not believe that I have ever violated that treaty; but [the government] never fulfilled its promises.[52]

Geronimo and his followers were put on a train and taken to dungeons in old Fort Pickens on Santa Rosa Island in Florida's Pensacola Bay. At Fort Marion, Geronimo's followers and other Chiricahua Apache were forced to live on an overcrowded, swampy reservation where great numbers of Native Americans succumbed to malaria. Children were snatched away from their mothers to learn how to live as white people. Their hair was shorn off, they were given American names, and they were sent to Carlisle Indian School in Pennsylvania, where one-quarter of them died from tuberculosis.

Geronimo (first row, second from right) and other Chiricahua prisoners sit on an embankment near the railroad car that will transport them to Florida's Fort Pickens.

For several years the Apache were shunted from reservation to reservation, and Geronimo was never allowed to join his family. Finally, in October 1894, the Apache were reunited in Fort Sill, Oklahoma, where they were allowed to live in villages similar to those of their old bands. They farmed and raised cattle, but they continued to sicken and die from alcohol and disease.

The sixty-five-year-old Geronimo earned money at Fort Sill by manufacturing bows and arrows and by selling autographed photos of himself. His status as a fierce Apache warrior made him an American legend, and he appeared at countless fairs and expositions. Geronimo even rode a horse down Pennsylvania Avenue in

Geronimo on Display

Geronimo was one of the most feared Native American warriors in American history. After his final surrender in 1886, however, newspapers and books wrote of Geronimo's daring exploits and elevated the Apache warrior to the status of a legend. In the early years of the twentieth century, Geronimo took advantage of this and became a one-man traveling show. The Apache's appearance at a fair or exhibition guaranteed commercial success, and the old warrior was gracious and friendly to those who crowded around him.

His first appearance was at the Trans-Mississippi and International Exposition held in Omaha, Nebraska, in 1898. A number of other Native American men, women, and children were selected from the Fort Sill, Oklahoma, prisoners, but Geronimo was the main attraction. When his train stopped at stations on the journey to the fair, Geronimo stripped buttons from his coat and sold them for twenty-five cents each and sold his hat for five dollars. Between stations he sewed on more buttons and put on a new hat from a supply he had brought with him.

Geronimo next appeared at the Pan-American Exposition in Buffalo, New York, in 1901, where he was paid forty-five dollars a month. At the 1904 Louisiana Purchase Exposition in St. Louis, Missouri, Congress approved seventy thousand dollars for the Department of the Interior to set up an exhibition demonstrating the way Native Americans lived before they were subdued. Geronimo lived in the "Apache Village" in the fair's Indian Building. In the village, Geronimo had a booth where he made bows and arrows and sold autographed pictures for up to two dollars each. In St. Louis, as with the other fairs he attended, Geronimo was kept under strict supervision by U.S. marshals, although he was allowed to go on fair rides and to visit the midway.

CHIEF
GERONIMO
No.39

After his imprisonment, Geronimo earned money by appearing at fairs and expositions and by selling autographed photographs such as this one.

Washington, D.C., during the inaugural parade of President Theodore Roosevelt in 1904. The Apache chief later went on to become a well-paid public speaker at festivals and fairs.

All the while, however, Geronimo yearned to return to his homeland. In his autobiography, he writes,

> There is no climate or soil which, to my mind, is equal to that of Arizona. We could have plenty of good cultivating land, plenty of grass, plenty of timber and plenty of minerals in that land which the Almighty created for the Apaches. It is my land, my home, my fathers' land, to which I now ask to be allowed to return. I want to spend my last days there, to be buried among those mountains. If this could be I might die in peace, feeling my people, placed in their native homes, would increase in number, rather than diminish as at present, and that our name would not become extinct.[53]

Geronimo filed many requests with the U.S. government to be allowed to return home. They were never honored. He lived out his final days as an official prisoner of war on the Oklahoma reservation.

In 1908, after a bout of drinking in the town of Lawton, Geronimo fell from his horse and spent the chilly night sprawled in some damp grass. He contracted pneumonia and died on February 17, having never seen his beloved Arizona again.

With the release of his autobiography two years before his death, Geronimo became an enduring symbol of Native American pride and ferocity. In 1913 his people were finally released from their imprisonment, and 187 members of the Chiricahua band journeyed to New Mexico to live quietly among the Mescalero Apache.

CHAPTER 5

Crazy Horse

Life for nineteenth-century chiefs was a constant struggle against white intruders. This was especially true for Crazy Horse, a chief of the Hunkpatila band of the Oglala Sioux, a tribe of buffalo hunters who roamed the plains in present-day Wyoming, Montana, South Dakota, and the panhandle of Nebraska. Crazy Horse valued his people's freedom above all else. He never signed a treaty, and he resisted white settlement of Indian lands for most of his life.

What is known about the life of Crazy Horse has been passed down from generation to generation by great grandfathers and great grandmothers who still talk of this Native American legend.

The Oglala Sioux were members of the Lakota people. They were related to six other Lakota Sioux tribes—the Brulé, the Hunkpapa, the Miniconjou, the Two Kettles, the Sans Arc, and the Blackfoot.

By the time of Crazy Horse's birth, sometime around the fall of 1841, wave after wave of white miners, ranchers, and farmers were streaming into Lakota territory. It became the duty of the U.S. Army to protect the frontier and to remove the Native Americans who stood in the way of white settlement.

Growing Up Lakota

Crazy Horse was born at a place called Bear Butte, just northeast of the Black Hills in South Dakota. His father, who was also named Crazy Horse, was a medicine man who taught his son to respect the powers of the Great Spirit. Although a full-blooded Oglala, the young boy's complexion was much fairer than his tribespeople. Since his hair was light brown and grew out in soft waves, he was given nicknames such as Light-Haired Boy, Curly Hair, or, more often, Curly.

In Russell Freedman's *The Life and Death of Crazy Horse*, a friend of Crazy Horse's named Short Bull remembers the chief's appearance:

Crazy Horse had a very light complexion, much lighter than the other Indians. . . . His features were not like those of the rest of us. His face was not broad, and he had a sharp, high nose. He had black eyes that hardly ever looked straight at a man, but they didn't miss much that was going on all the same.[54]

Like all Oglala babies, Curly was rubbed with buffalo fat for warmth and protection from rashes and infection. He was carried around in a cradle board on his mother's back and wore a diaper made from moss. If he cried loudly, his mother would quiet him with a sharp pinch to the nose. The Hunkpatila band often traveled through enemy territory—both white and Indian—and lessons in silence were given early and often.

Crazy Horse, the brave chief of the Hunkpatila band of Oglala Sioux, tried to preserve his tribes' freedom and lands.

As Curly grew, all of the band's lodges were open to him, as all Sioux children were fed and cuddled by the entire tribe. He addressed his parents as well as his aunts and uncles as "father" and "mother," and all tribe elders were considered "grandparents."

The Oglala, like the other tribes of the Great Plains, were constantly on the move. They might move twice a week in the spring to allow their pony herds to graze on fresh grasses. In the summer they followed the great swarms of buffalo as they moved to fresh pasture. When the Oglala were not hunting, they practiced their tradition of warfare, raiding the camps of enemy tribes such as the Pawnee, Omaha, and Shoshone. Warm summer nights were spent gathered with friendly bands dancing around fires, feasting, telling stories, and trading.

Most Oglala boys dreamed of becoming a great warrior or chief someday. In this, Curly was no different. As a teen, he would slip out of his tepee at night and follow older warriors as they went off to battle. Curly was allowed to come along, but he had to fetch water, tend horses, and stay behind to look after the camp during battles.

Song and Dance

The Sioux were fond of social gatherings that featured dance, song, food, games, and displays of finery, but religious ceremonies were most important. Luther Standing Bear elaborates in Land of the Spotted Eagle.

"[A] Lakota lived his aesthetic life through ceremonies, for they embodied his love for song, music, dance, rhythm, grace of motion, prayer, chant, ritualism, color, body decoration, and symbolic design. Tribal culture culminated in ceremony. . . .

Ceremonies were held for all main events of life—for birth . . . entrance into lodges, consecration to service, in celebration of victory, and for the giving of thanks. Contrary to general thought, less attention was paid to war in these ceremonies than anything else. Most of them were for the purpose of giving thanks for food, health, and like comforts. . . .

Since song was the usual method of keeping the Lakota in touch with his Wakan Tanka [Great Spirit], it formed a large part of all ritual. Many songs were dreamer songs received while in communion with spirits. . . .

Dancing was just as much a part of the Lakota's life and its meaning as song, and with dances he expressed the same emotions as he did with song—sorrow, bravery, ecstasy, valor, love, supplication, and devotion. Still other dances were enactments of past history, such as adventures, travel experiences, and battles. Another class of dances were named after . . . certain animals, showing his love for and dependence upon the animal kingdom, such as the Fox, Horse, and Buffalo dances."

Donning buffalo heads, Lakota warriors partake in the ritualistic Buffalo Dance.

Curly's Vision

Inspired by his father's teachings, Curly sought a spiritual vision that would distinguish him as a leader. Native American boys and girls of Curly's age often went by themselves to secluded places where they would commune with the sacred powers. The young people were questing for a vision that would guide them throughout their lives. Before a young person went on a vision quest, he or she would fast, spend long hours in a makeshift sauna called a sweat lodge, and ask a shaman for guidance.

When Curly was about thirteen, he went off on his vision quest undergoing the usual preparations and without counsel from a shaman or any other tribe elder. In spite of this, Curly received the vision that would guide him throughout his life—a vision that has been recounted hundreds of times in Sioux legend.

After several days of fasting and fighting off sleep on a hilltop, Curly entered the spirit world and saw his horse coming to him carrying a man with long brown hair. The horse changed colors and seemed to be floating above the ground. The rider's face was unpainted, and he had a hawk's feather in his hair and a small brown stone tied behind one ear. He spoke no words, but Curly heard his thoughts.

The rider told Curly that the young man must never wear a traditional war bonnet, paint his horse, or tie up its tail before going into battle, as other warriors did. Instead, Curly should sprinkle the horse with dust and rub dust on his own hair and body. Unlike victors who looted a vanquished enemy's possessions after a battle, Curly was never to take anything for himself. During Curly's vision, the horse and rider seemed to be surrounded by a shadow enemy. Arrows and bullets streaked toward the rider but fell to the ground without inflicting harm. A crowd of tribespeople appeared around the long-haired rider. They clutched at him to hold him back, but the rider rode off. A fierce storm blew up and hail spotted the rider's body and lightning zig-zagged across his cheek. The storm faded and a red-backed hawk flew over the rider's head.

The vision faded and Curly felt someone shaking him. It was his father, angry that the boy had ridden out by himself and without counsel, causing great worry among the Hunkpatila.

Curly did not tell his father of the spirit rider for several months. When he did, old Crazy Horse interpreted the dream. He said the phantom warrior was the man Curly would become. If Curly followed the rider's example and dressed as he had, never taking scalps or other prizes for himself, he would never be struck by enemy bullets or arrows. Old Crazy Horse believed Curly had been given powerful medicine and told his son to use it wisely so that he could one day lead his people, help the weak, and provide for the hungry.

The Grattan Massacre

Meanwhile, countless skirmishes, raids, and all-out battles were being fought between the people of the plains and white settlers and soldiers. In 1854 a Brulé warrior shot a Mormon settler's sick cow and ate it. The cow's owner complained to John L. Grattan, a senior officer at Fort Laramie. The twenty-four-year-old lieutenant, along with twenty soldiers and a cannon, confronted the Brulé tribespeople. To avoid trouble, the Brulé chief agreed to pay the settler twenty-five dollars for the cow—twice what it was worth. Grattan declined the offer, saying he wanted the chief to hand over the warrior who had killed the cow so that he could be put on trial in

The Treaty of 1851

In 1849, when Crazy Horse was about eight years old, gold was discovered in California. The Oregon Trail, which passed through the southern hunting grounds of the Sioux, suddenly filled with a steady stream of covered wagons heading to the gold rush. Although white settlers had used the Oregon Trail since 1841, the wagon trains now grew much longer, their white canvas tops swaying for miles as they stirred up clouds of choking dust.

The presence of so many white people caused great resentment among the Sioux. The only trees that grew on the Great Plains were the cottonwood that shaded river banks where the Sioux had camped for centuries. The settlers quickly cut these trees down to provide fuel for cooking and heating fires.

In 1851 the U.S. government called over ten thousand Native Americans to a council at Fort Laramie, Wyoming. Government agents showered their guests with gifts, hoping to win their favor and get them to sign treaties. The government proposals were far-reaching: Officials wanted to divide the Great Plains into separate territories and assign different bands to each region. Tribes were asked not to cross the borders of their own district or to wage war on other tribes. Likewise, each tribe was asked to pick a leader who could speak for the entire tribe. White settlers, however, would be allowed to cross the lands.

Some Native Americans—including the Oglala Sioux—refused to sign, but after a few weeks of pressure, cajoling, and threats, a majority of other Sioux leaders approved the treaty.

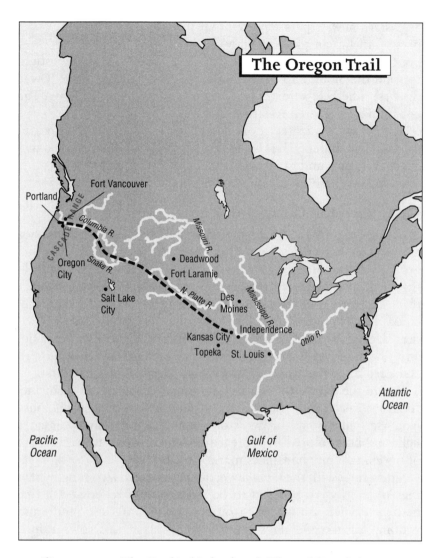

a military court. The Brulé chief refused. The soldiers left, warning the Brulé that they would soon be back to exact justice.

The Brulé went to the Oglala Sioux to tell them what had happened. Both tribes prepared for war. On August 19 thirty-one soldiers came to the Brulé camp. As the thirteen-year-old Curly watched, the Brulé chief offered the best ponies in the Indian herd to the owner of the dead cow. Grattan ignored the chief, demanding the immediate arrest of the cow's killer. After a tense standoff, the army unit, wielding a twelve-pound cannon, opened fire. Several Brulé died, including the chief, and a fight began. Grattan was killed, his body pierced by twenty-four arrows. The rest of the soldiers were killed in a matter of minutes.

Eastern newspapers reported that the "Grattan Massacre" was part of an Indian plot. The cow had not been killed for its meat but to lure innocent soldiers out of their fort. An army investigator said the Sioux had deliberately ambushed the soldiers. It was the first time U.S. soldiers had been killed by Plains Indians. The government prepared to strike back.

The army instigated dozens of raids on Native American camps. The Indians retaliated by raiding wagon trains, stagecoaches, farms, and ranches. Crazy Horse, who was now a young man, joined these raids as a warrior in training.

Curly Becomes Crazy Horse

In the summer of 1858 Curly had learned the ways of the warrior and was ready to prove himself in battle. By that time the hunting grounds of the Sioux had been depleted by settlers. The buffalo that had once darkened the prairies were now so few in number that the Sioux could no longer survive in their traditional homelands. They were forced to move their hunting camps to the Powder River in Wyoming, where their enemies, the Crow, Arapaho, and Shoshone tribes, lived. Instead of waiting for an attack to come from the enemy tribes, the Oglala decided to strike first.

Before the battle, Curly carefully prepared his battle medicine. As in the vision, he wore a red-backed hawk feather in his loose hair. He tied a small brown stone behind his ear and painted a lightning bolt colored by red earth from his forehead to the base of his chin. White hail spots marked his body.

Curly rode with the Oglala warriors to central Wyoming, where the Arapaho were believed to be peaceful and to possess a fine herd of ponies. As it turned out, the Arapaho were ready and waiting for the Oglala warriors. Guns blasted, arrows rained down, and the Oglala dug in for battle.

After about two hours, with little progress on either side, the Oglala Sioux prepared to retreat. Curly's vision told him otherwise, however. He caught the reins of a pony and charged through a hail of Arapaho arrows and bullets. Untouched, he drove an arrow through an Arapaho warrior, killing him. Curly turned and charged again, this time killing a second warrior with a blast from his pistol.

The Oglala warrior slipped off his pony and took the scalps of the men he killed, but he was quickly struck in the leg with an arrow. Curly found shelter behind a rock, and a friend wrapped his wound with fresh skin stripped from a dead horse. Taking the scalps had been a mistake—the rider in his vision had warned him

Traditional Warfare

The traditional Native American methods of warfare did not involve mass killings. Most Native Americans were eager to demonstrate their own courage and were less interested in exacting total defeat upon an enemy. Typical battles between tribes rarely produced more than a dozen casualties.

Warriors went into battle with guns and bows and arrows, but they saw scant honor in using these deadly weapons, since it did not require much courage to strike an enemy from a distance. It was considered far braver to kill an enemy with a knife or a war club.

Native American warriors gained prestige by "counting coup." This involved getting close enough to an enemy to strike him with a lance, bare hand, or coup stick (a tool made especially for this purpose). The highest honors were given to Sioux warriors who confiscated an enemy's weapon, rescued a friend in the heat of battle, or received a wound in combat.

Little honor was seen in destroying an enemy's army, though. A missionary who lived among the Santee Sioux from 1835 to 1845 documented the Santee's constant combat with four other tribes. During those ten years, the missionary noted only 88 Sioux casualties and 129 enemy losses.

The Sioux believed that American soldiers lacked courage because they preferred to fight from far distances while hiding behind earthen embankments. Likewise, the Native Americans were astounded at the white men's desire to completely wipe out every last Indian in combat, including women and children.

After fighting white soldiers, however, Native Americans began to adopt many of the army's tactics and used them when battling the whites.

to avoid taking anything for himself during battle. From that day forward, he would not ignore the messages delivered by his spirit rider.

The Oglala continued the attack and returned home victorious. They had killed four enemy warriors, counted many coups, taken some good horses, and not lost a single brave. Curly's charge had turned the battle in the Oglala's favor. When a victory dance was held, Curly remained stoic and silent. The next morning, old Crazy Horse strode through the village singing the praises of his son:

My son has been against people of an unknown tongue.
He has done a brave thing;
for this I give him a new name, the name of his father,

and of many fathers before him—
I give him a great name.
I call him Crazy Horse.[55]

A procession of people followed behind old Crazy Horse, stopping at the lodge where young Crazy Horse resided. Almost the
entire village had come to revere him for his brave deed in battle.
Well into the night, old men, women, children, warriors, shamans,
and chiefs sang, danced, and feasted in honor of their new warrior
and subchief Crazy Horse. When the feast was over, Crazy Horse
undertook the task of training his followers in the art of war.

Hit-and-Run Warfare

In 1865 the U.S. government offered the people of the Great
Plains another in a long series of treaties. This one seemed accept-
able to the Native Americans; it bequeathed to them all the lands
known as the Powder River Country, located between the Black
Hills, the Yellowstone River, and the Rocky Mountains. These
were the finest buffalo hunting grounds on the plains.

The Black Hills, called Paha Sapa, were sacred to the Sioux.
They were a place where game flourished, pine trees swayed in the
wind, and ancestral spirits lived. The hills were a source of lodge-
pole pine, which were used for tepees; of medicinal plants; and the
home to the Great Spirit—all that was powerful and sacred. White
leaders promised the Powder River Country to the Sioux "as long
as the grass shall grow and the waters flow." [56]

Crazy Horse counseled others not to trust the white men's
treaty, and soon his suspicions were proven correct. Before a year
had passed, gold was discovered in Montana and Idaho, and a
new wave of white people came streaming into the Powder River
Country. The Bureau of Indian Affairs (also known as the Indian
Agency) in Washington, D.C., demanded a new treaty that would
allow the government to build roads and forts in the area. Crazy
Horse refused and told the commander at Fort Laramie that the
whites must honor the treaty or prepare to fight.

Federal officials in faraway Washington had no interest in forcing out white settlers and miners, so Indian demands for adhering
to the treaty were ignored. Colonel Henry B. Carrington was ordered to build the Bozeman Trail directly through the Powder
River Country to Montana and to construct a line of forts to protect the trail. The first fort built was called Fort Phil Kearny.

Crazy Horse fought back. His braves ambushed wagon trains
and began shooting at small groups of soldiers when they were

After whites failed to honor treaties with their Native American neigh-bors, Crazy Horse and his warriors retaliated by attacking wagon trains passing through their territory.

out alone on patrol. At the same time, Crazy Horse gathered a war party of one thousand men from the Arapaho, Cheyenne, Hunkpapa, and Miniconjou tribes. These warriors were joined by about one thousand Oglala warriors.

Most of the skirmishes between the Sioux and the U.S. Army were centered around Fort Kearny, which was surrounded by miles of treeless prairie. The only timber that the fort could use for firewood was six miles away. Every two weeks woodcutting parties left the fort with an escort of cavalry to cut the timber. On a cold December morning, Crazy Horse hid a few warriors to take potshots at the woodcutters while they were still close to the fort. The troopers screamed for help and Colonel Carrington quickly sent a relief party of eighty-one cavalrymen to rescue the woodcutters.

The soldiers charged past the wood train and went after the dozen or so Native Americans crouched among the rocks in the narrow ravine. They ran directly into an ambush. Hundreds of warriors appeared and in less than half an hour, all of the soldiers were dead.

For the next six months Crazy Horse and his warriors continued with random, surprise attacks, making life miserable for the remaining soldiers in Fort Kearny. Throughout this time Crazy Horse remained true to his boyhood vision. According to *Crazy Horse: The Strange Man of the Oglalas,*

Now more than ever, the Oglalas spoke of Crazy Horse as their Strange Man. [After being slightly wounded in battle] his skin [looked] even lighter, and his hair seemed to have grown longer . . . the brown, fur-wrapped braids hanging far below his belt. It seemed he went about the village a little oftener to see that there was meat in the kettles, a horse for every travois. His dress was plain as ever and his passing more silent than the summer wind.[57]

Gold in the Sacred Black Hills

In the summer of 1868, unexpected news came across the telegraph lines. The federal government wanted to draw up another Powder River treaty. The new terms promised gifts to those Native Americans who would move to reservations. Although Crazy Horse refused, about half of the northern Oglala Sioux moved to a plot of land surrounded by government buildings near Fort Laramie.

Crazy Horse and Sitting Bull (chief of the Hunkpapa Sioux) said they would only sign the treaty if the army closed all forts in the region and left the land to the Native Americans. Surprisingly, the Indian Agency agreed, and the forts were abandoned. After the last of the soldiers left, Crazy Horse ordered all the stockades burned to the ground.

Chief Sitting Bull, pictured here sometime around 1880, joined forces with Crazy Horse.

The Treaty of 1868 created a large reservation for the Sioux in the Dakota Territory, stretching from the Missouri River (in present-day North and South Dakota) to the Black Hills. It also established Indian agencies where various bands could receive government rations and trading with whites could take place. The Oglala band was ordered onto a spot far from the Powder River Country, but many Sioux did not observe the treaty and continued to live in their traditional homelands.

For several years white soldiers avoided the Powder River Country, and the Sioux lived in peace. In 1874, however, a few prospectors ventured into the sacred Black Hills and discovered gold. This caused concern among Native Americans, who believed that "even the sight of one of those [gold] stones would bring a burning to the brain of the white man, a craziness."[58] Until this time, settlers had considered the Black Hills, with its rocky soil and steep slopes, to be worthless. Now, almost overnight, gold-hungry prospectors flooded into the area.

Refusing to Surrender

The U.S. government did nothing to stop the gold hunters or to enforce the Powder River treaty. Orders were sent that all Native Americans were to leave the Great Plains and move to reservations. Money was offered to the tribes for their land—money that would never be paid. Those who did not come to the Indian agencies would be considered hostile and would be hunted down like animals.

Many of the chiefs decided that fighting was hopeless and surrendered. One of those chiefs, Red Cloud, was honored by the Indian Agency, which named the Red Cloud Reservation in South Dakota after him. This influenced hundreds of Sioux to peacefully move onto the reservation; however, Crazy Horse and other warriors were saddened by Red Cloud's concessions to the whites.

Crazy Horse, who was now the head chief of the Oglala Sioux, retreated to the hills with his warriors and their families. They were joined by Sitting Bull and his warriors as well as by Native Americans from other Indian bands who also refused to give up their freedom.

The thought of several thousand warriors in one place alarmed government authorities, who assembled a fighting force of thirty-five hundred handpicked veterans to wipe out Crazy Horse and his warriors. They moved into the Powder River Country under the command of General George Crook in 1876.

Sioux chief Red Cloud voluntarily moved his tribe to a reservation in South Dakota.

Crook sent the Seventh Cavalry into the Powder River Country to round up the Sioux and either force them onto the reservation or kill them. The cavalry was under the command of General George Armstrong Custer, a flamboyant Civil War hero whose long blond curls fell down over his fringed buckskin jackets. The Sioux called him Long Hair. Custer's Seventh Cavalry, which consisted of about six hundred mounted troopers, was well-armed with Colt revolvers and lightweight short rifles called carbines. The Seventh also employed about thirty-five Native American scouts from the Crow and Arikara tribes.

Custer's Last Stand

On June 24, as the army pressed deep into the Powder River region, Crook sent Custer's forces to scout ahead and find the location of Crazy Horse and Sitting Bull. Crook warned Custer not to attack until the entire army was in place and offered Custer the use of the Second Cavalry to act as reinforcements. Custer turned down the offer, boasting, "I could whip all the Indians on the continent with the Seventh Cavalry." [59]

Early the next morning Custer found a village of Native Americans in the valley of the Little Bighorn River. On this hot summer day, children were splashing in the river, women were talking and working, and the men were smoking and tending to their weapons. Custer believed he was observing the entire village, but several hundred tepees were hidden behind bluffs and trees.

Disobeying Crook's orders, Custer decided to attack the village immediately. He divided his command and ordered Major Marcus A. Reno to lead three companies directly to the Little Bighorn River, where they would cross the stream and attack the village from the south. Custer would lead five companies along the high bluffs and attack the northern edge of the village.

With a volley of carbine bullets ripping into the tepees, Reno's men charged at a group of Hunkpapa lodges. Crazy Horse's men suddenly swarmed down the hills behind the cavalry. Reno signaled a retreat, but it was too late. When the battle was over, 40 of Reno's 140 men lay dead, 13 were wounded, and 17 were stranded below. Warriors began shooting at the stragglers, but Sitting Bull said, "Let them go . . . so they can tell the whites what happened!" [60]

Suddenly the Native Americans caught sight of Custer's blue column of soldiers on a high ridge above the river. The warriors left Reno's troops to attack the new enemy.

As Custer's soldiers galloped toward the river bank, hundreds of warriors converged on the spot to fight them. As planned, Sitting

Bull rounded up the children, women, and elders to take them to safety. At the same time, Crazy Horse, who had not yet made it into battle, swept through the village gathering warriors.

The battle did not last long. Custer tried to retreat to the safety of the hilltop, but it was occupied by the Sioux. The Seventh Cavalry was forced to fight on the hillside. When the final rifle was fired and the last arrow was shot, possibly two hours after Reno's initial charge, the entire Seventh Cavalry—264 men, including Custer—lay dead.

Throughout the battle Crazy Horse acted with ferocious bravery. The vision he had experienced at age thirteen carried him through this battle as it had done in so many other fights. Charles Fire Thunder, a Lakota Sioux born in 1909, describes the legendary bullet magic of Crazy Horse:

> Once in a while [during the Battle of Little Bighorn] Crazy Horse would expose himself to the soldiers, so they could take a good aim and shoot at him. . . . Custer and his men were completely wiped out in less than a day. The reason was, Crazy Horse was the commander of these warriors that fought Custer. On account of Crazy Horse, white soldiers or enemies could not take advantage of his people. He was a courageous man, for he knew himself that in war there was no weapon that would harm him.[61]

Surrounded by the superior forces of Crazy Horse and Sitting Bull, cavalry commander George Armstrong Custer (center) fights his last battle.

A Bayonet in the Back

After the victory at Little Bighorn, in order to drive off evil spirits and gain powerful medicine, the bodies of the Seventh Cavalry soldiers were stripped, plundered, and mutilated. Confident that the Sioux had taught the army a lesson, Sitting Bull and Crazy Horse believed they would be free to move about the Powder River hunting grounds. The American public and its leaders, however, were bent on revenge.

Custer's Last Stand, as it was called, shocked and humiliated Americans. It was the biggest loss ever suffered by the U.S. Army at the hands of Native Americans. Newspapers and politicians called for immediate revenge. As the residents of the Native American village on the Little Bighorn scattered to find new hunting grounds, the Indians learned that the army was coming after them. Crazy Horse and Sitting Bull decided it would be best to break up their forces. Sitting Bull took his Hunkpapa warriors into Canada, and Crazy Horse led the Oglala band deep into the Black Hills.

After Crazy Horse and his followers set up camp in the Black Hills, they learned that Red Cloud and some other chiefs had sold the sacred hills to the United States, thus giving up all rights to the hunting grounds.

Following the crushing defeat at Little Bighorn, the U.S. cavalry heightened its efforts to round up renegade Native Americans.

Winter came, with temperatures dipping below zero, but the army continued to relentlessly pursue the Oglala, Cheyenne, and other tribes who had fought at Little Bighorn. The hungry, frozen Native Americans were forced to either fight or flee from the white soldiers, who were specially trained and equipped for winter fighting. In one skirmish, the army chased two hundred Cheyenne from their village, captured their ponies, and burned their tepees and possessions. For two agonizing weeks, the Cheyenne walked through the snow before taking refuge at Crazy Horse's camp.

The Oglala welcomed the Cheyenne and shared what little food they had, but the Native Americans began to sicken and starve in their snow-bound tepees. On New Year's Day, 1877, the army found the Oglala camp and attacked at dawn. Crazy Horse and his warriors held off the soldiers while the women and children fled to safety. For several days the soldiers followed the fleeing Oglala Sioux, attacking again and again. On January 8 the two sides fought for five hours in a blizzard. The army finally retreated, and Crazy Horse and several renegade bands continued to camp in the snow.

In April a Native American scout working for the U.S. government found Crazy Horse and delivered a message from Crook: If Crazy Horse would surrender, his Oglala tribespeople would be treated with mercy. Around him, Crazy Horse saw only starving people who were weakened from a freezing winter. He knew the end had come. Finally he led his followers on a last long march to the Red Cloud Reservation. The Bureau of Indian Affairs declared that Crazy Horse was to be arrested upon his arrival at the reservation. Following his arrest, he was to be imprisoned for life in a federal prison camp on Dry Tortugas Island, located off the coast of Florida.

When Crazy Horse arrived at Red Cloud, none of the officers told him this information; they simply asked him to visit the reservation's commanding officer. Once he was inside the officer's barracks, however, he saw that the windows were covered with bars. Crazy Horse realized he was in jail. With a war whoop, he broke away from the soldiers who were escorting him. One of the soldiers lunged forward with his bayonet and sank it deep between the war chief's ribs. Crazy Horse was dead.

The next morning Crazy Horse was buried in the reservation graveyard. But later that night, some Oglala people dug up his body, laid him over the back of a pony, slipped past the guards, and headed into the Black Hills. No one knows where Crazy Horse is buried, but the site is believed to be somewhere in the sacred hunting grounds that the warrior tried to save for his people.

CHAPTER 6

Wilma Mankiller

The victory of Crazy Horse and his Sioux people over General George Custer was the last such success for Native Americans in the United States. By the 1900s, most were living on reservations located in isolated and desolate regions, on lands no one else wanted. Other Native Americans struggled to make lives in cities and towns far from the wilderness that had sustained them and their ancestors. Meanwhile, the prairie was fenced off and farmed by white settlers, and trains and roads crisscrossed the wilderness. Forests were also clear-cut and turned into timber for houses and newspapers.

In spite of the wars, relocations, and diseases, several hundred thousand Native American people were still alive in America. One of the families that had been forced onto a reservation in Oklahoma was the Mankillers, descendants of Cherokee warriors. A granddaughter by the name of Wilma would one day bring fame to the Mankillers—and their ancestors who had once thrived in the North American wilderness.

Wilma Mankiller, the only female ever elected chief of the Cherokee Nation.

Born into Poverty

Wilhelmina Mankiller was born on November 18, 1945, in the small town of Tahlequah, the capital of the Cherokee Nation in northeastern Oklahoma. Wilma was the sixth of eleven children in her family. Her mother was Dutch-Irish, and her father was a Cherokee Indian.

Native American Names

The name Mankiller, *or* Asgaya-dihi *in Cherokee, was used by Wilma Mankiller's family for four generations. Although it is an old Cherokee name, at one time it was a rank or title such as major or captain, and it was used only after someone had earned the right to use it by killing a man. In her autobiography* Mankiller, *the Cherokee chief talks about the Indian tradition of names.*

"Native Americans regard their names not as mere labels, but as essential parts of their personalities. A native person's name is as vital to his or her identity as the eyes or teeth. There is a common belief that when a person is injured, her name is maligned, just as she might be bruised when in an accident....

If prayers and medicine fail to heal the seriously ill person, the spiritual leader sometimes realizes that the patient's name itself may be diseased. The priest then goes to the water and, with the appropriate ceremony, bestows a new name on the sick person."

Wilma spent her early years at Mankiller Flatts, a 160-acre parcel first obtained by her paternal grandfather. Her house—which she remembers as very small and crowded—was built by her father, uncle, and oldest brother. Like many of their Cherokee neighbors, the Mankillers lived without any modern conveniences in conditions of extreme poverty. According to Mankiller,

That house had been built of rough lumber and had four rooms, all with bare plank floors and walls. It was covered by a tin roof. In the winter, the only heat came from a wood stove. That is also how we cooked. There was no electricity, and we used coal-oil lamps to light the rooms. We had a few pieces of furniture. There was an outhouse for a toilet. Mom used a wringer washer with a gasoline motor. . . . For washing and cooking, we had to haul water from the spring a quarter mile from the house. The spring also served as a refrigerator for some of our food. We kept a box in the cold water to hold the milk and other perishables. . . .

Like many of the people [of the Cherokee Nation] we were "dirt poor. . . ." In the late 1940s and the 1950s, the Cherokee population . . . lived in extreme poverty in Cherokee communities such as ours, scattered throughout the hills. Those settlements did not appear on any maps.

Many of them were not visible from the road to travelers passing through the area. Each community was made up of families living on their individual allotments of land.

People tended to congregate for various events at a community center or a church or school, or one of the tribal ceremonial grounds where dances were held.[62]

Although most of the residents of Tahlequah came from Cherokee/white ancestry, most of them spoke the Cherokee language in their homes and as their first language. Some spoke no English at all. Street signs were in English and Cherokee, and the town even had a Cherokee-language Baptist church. In the Mankiller home, the two languages were used interchangeably. Mankiller's white mother learned enough Cherokee to hold a simple conversation.

Mankiller attended a three-room schoolhouse from first to fifth grade. Most of her clothing consisted of hand-me-downs or was made from recycled materials. "Our flour came in huge sacks," Mankiller writes, "so my mother used that cloth to make our clothes, both underwear and some of our outerwear."[63]

Leaving the Reservation

When Wilma was almost eleven years old, the Mankiller family left the country for the city in order to take advantage of a Bureau of Indian Affairs (BIA) program. The BIA was encouraging Native Americans to move from the reservations, where poverty and unemployment were rampant, to cities in which they could live and work, in Mankiller's words, "like white people."[64]

Although the program was aimed at improving the lives of Native Americans, Mankiller did not see it that way. When her family moved in 1956, she wrote that they said

> farewell to the land that had been our family's home for generations, and [moved] far away to a strange place. . . .
> It was then that I came to know in some small way what it was like for our ancestors when the government troops made them give up their houses and property. It was a time for me to be sad.[65]

The Mankillers moved to San Francisco, California. Wilma had never lived with plumbing or electricity, nor had she ever seen a television or traveled more than thirty miles from home. Although the BIA had promised her family an apartment, it was not available when they arrived. Her family was forced to move into a dirty hotel in the tenderloin district, an area notorious for its many dance

The Cherokee Nation

The Cherokee and the related tribes of the Choctaw, Chickasaw, Creek, and Seminole originally lived in Georgia, Tennessee, Virginia, and elsewhere in the Southeast. In the early nineteenth century, the state of Georgia began to grow rapidly around sovereign Cherokee lands—lands that were good for growing cotton and tobacco and where gold had been discovered.

In 1838 and 1839, the federal government compelled the Cherokee to walk across the country to the present-day state of Oklahoma. The route they took was known as "the Trail of Tears" because so many Cherokee died on this forced march, most of which was conducted during the winter.

When the Native Americans arrived in what was then called Indian Territory, they were given rights to nearly the entire region. The Cherokee took the northeastern corner of the state, and the tribe's new home was known as the Cherokee Nation. The treaty the Cherokee signed with the government, like so many others, promised that the Indians would own the lands forever.

In 1907 Indian sovereignty was destroyed when Oklahoma became a state. Land held in common by the Cherokee Nation was parceled out in individual allotments of 160 acres per family. Almost immediately the land was taken away by unscrupulous businessmen in shady land deals. This situation was aggravated by the discovery of oil in Oklahoma. The oil boom brought thousands of land swindlers, oil workers, and businessmen who took possession of Native American land titles in questionable deals.

At the time of the 1990 U.S. census, 308,132 Cherokee people lived in Oklahoma, with about 95,400 of them living on the reservation. Those who avoided the 1838 removal escaped into the Great Smoky Mountains and resettled in North Carolina. About 10,000 Cherokee live on a reservation there.

After oil was discovered in Oklahoma, boomtowns like this one flourished on lands once held by the Cherokee.

clubs, prostitutes, homeless alcoholics, barking dogs, and wailing sirens. Mankiller, who had never heard a siren, was terrified—she thought it was the sound of wild creatures screaming.

Although the BIA made many promises to the Mankillers about the prosperity they would find if they left the reservation, the family received little help from the government agency and had difficulty adjusting to their new location. They were left on their own to struggle in the big city.

Life in San Francisco

After a few weeks the Mankiller family moved from the tenderloin district to a small apartment in a better neighborhood. Mankiller's father got a job paying forty-eight dollars a week, which was far too little to support a large family in San Francisco. Her brother also worked, and both men walked miles to and from their factory jobs every day. Before long the rent became too much, and the Mankillers moved to the Hunter's Point neighborhood, a multicultural neighborhood where drugs, crime, and street gangs dominated daily life.

As one of the few Native Americans in her neighborhood, Mankiller had a very difficult time being accepted. In school she was mercilessly teased for her last name. In a later interview, Mankiller spoke of problems faced by Native Americans in school:

> Many Native students in public schools have had wrenching experiences. They're teased about their names, called chief, or they're expected to be the authority on every Indian tribe and issue. That's a tremendous burden for a child. . . .
>
> I was, like so many Native children, teased about my name, my accent. I had a very tough time throughout my school years. I searched for role models in the history books but found very few. For years I had no self-esteem.[66]

Wilma was able to find relief from her problems at the San Francisco Indian Center, where she befriended other Native Americans, including many Cherokee from back home. For more than a dozen years of its existence, this center was a home away from home for as many as thirty thousand Native Americans. In a speech given in 1993 at Sweet Briar College in Virginia, Mankiller remembered the San Francisco Indian Center:

> What kept us together, I think, as a family during that period of time was the Indian center, which was a place where many other families like ours, sort of refugees, I

90

guess you could say in the city, gathered at the San Francisco Indian Center and shared our experiences and kind of tried to build a community there.[67]

A Lasting Influence

After Mankiller graduated from high school in June 1963, she moved out of her parents' house and took up residence with her sister. Mankiller got a day job with a finance company performing clerical work. On November 13, five days short of her eighteenth birthday, Mankiller married Hector Hugo Olay, an Ecuador native from her old neighborhood, whom she had been dating for several years. Mankiller's daughter, Felicia, was born nine months later. A second daughter, Gina, was born in 1966.

Shortly after the birth of her children, Mankiller moved from Hunter's Point to a nicer neighborhood in the Mission District. Although she had a family and a home, the twenty-one-year-old Mankiller felt that she was missing out on the great changes that were taking place all around her.

The early 1960s was an exciting time to live in the San Francisco area. Mankiller describes what was happening around her at the time:

At the "hungry i" and other local nightclubs, folk singers, balladeers, and comics performed. . . . Bob Dylan sang from the depths of his soul, and out of Carmel and Big Sur country emerged Joan Baez with her sweet laments. Abstract painters and sculptors, drawn to the city, turned to a new realism. It was a time when prose writers, poets and playwrights lived in "pads," experimented with pot, and practiced Zen. Each evening, they met at one of the city's many cafés or coffeehouses to sip espresso or glasses of golden Napa wine while devouring freshly composed poems. . . . Any self-respecting radical, nonconformist, or renegade knew the place to be was San Francisco.[68]

Protesters in San Francisco burn their draft cards during the social unrest of the 1960s.

Besides these changes, African Americans were gaining strength and becoming more vociferous in their demand for civil rights. In September 1966 devastating riots erupted in Hunter's Point following the police shooting of a seventeen-year-old African-American male. The Black Power movement inspired Hispanic leaders to speak out, and people of all colors were taking to the streets to protest the war in Vietnam. According to Mankiller, "Everything that was happening in the world at that time—Vietnam, peace demonstrations, the civil-rights movement, and the seeds of the native rights movement had a lasting influence on me."[69]

The atmosphere of protest and change was gripping the Native American community. In 1968 a new era of Native American militancy began with the founding of the American Indian Movement (AIM). AIM chapters soon appeared on reservations and in cities across the country. Members demonstrated and staged sit-ins to protest the loss of tribal lands and resources. The San Francisco Indian Center was the center for this movement in the Bay Area.

Seizing Alcatraz

In November 1969 eighty-nine Native Americans occupied Alcatraz Island in San Francisco Bay. Citing a clause in a forgotten treaty that said any unused federal lands must revert to Indian use, the Native Americans took over the twelve-acre island, which was the location of the infamous Alcatraz Federal Prison until 1963. This move by AIM drew worldwide media attention.

After occupying San Francisco's Alcatraz Island, members of AIM inspect the abandoned cell blocks of the infamous federal prison.

The American Indian Movement (AIM)

The American Indian Movement (AIM) is an organization dedicated to reminding the U.S. government to uphold treaties and other obligations to Indian people. The organization was founded in Minneapolis, Minnesota, in 1968 by Clyde and Virgil Bellecourt, Charles Mitchell, and Dennis Banks, all members of the Ojibwa tribe; and Russell Means, an Oglala Sioux. The organization's first mission was to observe police patrols in Indian neighborhoods where there had been reports of police harassment. With AIM monitoring, reports of problems by the police dropped sharply.

After this success AIM concerned itself with Indian issues such as unemployment and substandard housing. It conducted nonviolent protests and generated substantial media attention for its efforts. This publicity led to more followers, and AIM opened offices in other cities. From 1969 to 1971 AIM members occupied Alcatraz, the former prison island in San Francisco Bay. This move attracted worldwide publicity for the Indian cause.

Other occupations followed, with AIM demanding that Indian tribes be recognized as independent, sovereign nations as spelled out by existing treaties with the United States. In 1971 AIM occupied Mount Rushmore, the granite memorial to American presidents in the Black Hills.

In 1973 the little town of Wounded Knee, South Dakota, located in the Pine Ridge Reservation, became the site of a major AIM protest. Two hundred armed AIM members took control of the village and demanded that the U.S. Senate investigate 371 Indian treaties that had been broken by the U.S. government. Federal law enforcement officials surrounded the town in a siege that lasted seventy-one days. Two Indians were killed, and one federal marshal was left paralyzed before the standoff ended.

The demonstrators held the island for the next nineteen months. As word of the protest spread, the population of the island sometimes swelled to over one thousand Native Americans who represented twenty tribes. They came from every region of the United States, bringing food, ceremonial items, and prayer. America's rich and famous also joined the protest, including Anthony Quinn, Jane Fonda, Jonathan Winters, Merv Griffin, and Candice Bergen. Politicians, reporters, Black Panthers, Girl Scout troops, and members of women's groups braved Coast Guard blockades to protest on Alcatraz with the Native Americans.

Mankiller also joined the protesters on the island. She says that becoming involved with the Alcatraz takeover forever changed her. In a 1993 speech, Mankiller remembers,

> My family became very involved in that movement, and so from that point on, I became very, very interested and I acquired skills because I wanted to help my own people. So I figured out how to organize things. I figured out how to do paralegal work. I was encouraged to go to college. Nobody in my family went to college—nobody I knew went to college. Certainly no one in Hunter's Point, the housing project I lived in, went to college. It was conceptually out of our space. And this one woman . . . who always thought I had leadership potential and didn't just see a ghetto kid, talked me into going to college.[70]

In June 1971 federal marshals removed the last of the occupants from Alcatraz. By then Mankiller had a new outlook on life, inspired by her work on Alcatraz. Her experiences there changed how she perceived herself as a Cherokee and as a woman. She writes about that period of her life: "Every day that passed seemed to give me more self-respect and sense of pride."[71]

Going Home

In 1971 Mankiller's father, Charles, died from kidney disease at the age of fifty-six. The family buried him in Oklahoma, and Mankiller returned to the land of her birth to attend the funeral. Even in her grief, Mankiller took comfort in returning to Mankiller Flatts. She was able to once again visit with her relatives and old friends who remained in the area. When Mankiller was driving back to San Francisco after the funeral, she began to think about returning to the land of her birth.

Back in California, Mankiller continued her participation in Native American causes and began to attend San Francisco State University. She also became the director of the Native American Youth Center in East Oakland, where she helped young people cope with life in the city. Mankiller volunteered for other Native American causes and worked for a time with several native California tribes in the northern part of the state. While working with these tribes, Mankiller came to realize that she needed to return to Oklahoma:

> More and more, I found my eyes turning away from the sea and the setting sun. I looked to the east where the sun begins its daily journey. That was where I had to go. . . . I

had to go back to stay. Back to the land of my birth, back to the soil and the trees my grandfather had touched. . . . The circle had been completed. It was so simple, so easy.

I was going home.[72]

Mankiller's husband had not supported her during the Alcatraz takeover, and the couple seemed headed in two different directions. Mankiller divorced her husband and went back to Oklahoma in 1977. Her first job was to enroll Native American youths in a national environmental studies program, which was funded by the U.S. Department of Labor.

Car Crashes and Disease

In 1979 Mankiller decided to continue her college education. She attended the University of Arkansas at Fayetteville to earn a bachelor of science degree. At the university, Mankiller studied community planning, social programs, architecture, and engineering, all fields that she believed would help her solve problems in the Cherokee community.

One morning Mankiller decided to skip school in order to talk to the personnel director of the Cherokee Nation about part-time work. On her drive into Tahlequah, Mankiller topped a hill on a rural road and saw that another car was coming at her in her lane. The two automobiles met in a head-on collision. The hood of Mankiller's car cut into her neck. Her face was crushed along with her right leg. Her left leg and ankle were broken, as were many of her ribs. The woman who had hit her died in the wreck.

After six hours in surgery, Mankiller was put in intensive care. The road to recovery was a long one, and Mankiller depended on Cherokee healing ceremonies and prayer to maintain a positive state of mind. The accident changed her life. As Mankiller writes, "From that point on, I have always thought of myself as the woman who lived before [the accident] and the woman who lives afterward."[73]

Mankiller began to experience severe health problems three months after the accident. She lost control of her muscles and could not maintain her grip on a pencil or a hairbrush. She began to experience double vision and could no longer walk on her crutches. After several weeks, Mankiller could only speak for short periods before her voice muscles would give out. Barely able to get out of bed to eat, Mankiller lost forty pounds.

Ten months after the accident, Mankiller learned that her physical difficulties were caused by a condition called myasthenia gravis. A form of muscular dystrophy that can lead to paralysis, myasthenia gravis can be controlled through surgery and medication. Mankiller's doctors recommended both. The operation and medicine restored her health; though she still experiences muscular dysfunction, she controls it with medication.

The Community Planner

After her recovery Mankiller went back to work. She believed housing and water problems were the biggest obstacles facing the Cherokee Nation. Under the direction of Chief Ross Swimmer, Mankiller organized the Department of Community Development. Her job involved building with concrete and steel but she also focused on the human side of her work. She asked for community input in her projects, taking suggestions from the people who would benefit from the projects. Mankiller wanted to prove that Native Americans could solve their own problems.

Her first project, started in 1981, was in the Cherokee community of Bell, where 110 families lived. More than one quarter of those families had no indoor plumbing, and people still had to hunt to find enough food to eat. The average elder lived on less than fifteen-hundred dollars a year.

Mankiller and community activist Charlie Soap (who would later become her husband) oversaw the project. With the construction of a sixteen-mile pipeline, the homes of Bell citizens were equipped with running water. Mankiller describes the project:

> We . . . recruited many volunteers to allow local citizens to construct . . . [the] water line and to revitalize several of their homes. In my mind, the Bell project remains a shining example of community self-help at its very best. The local residents were able to build on our Cherokee . . . tradition of physical sharing of tasks and work collectively, at the same time restoring confidence in their own ability to solve problems.[74]

By 1982 Mankiller was taking her expertise and compassion to other communities in the region.

Chief Mankiller

Mankiller's projects were so successful that people urged her to run for political office. She was uncomfortable with political demands such as making speeches and promoting herself, but she was eager to make decisions for her community without having to first ask someone else for approval. Mankiller discusses how she decided to run:

Housing conditions within the Cherokee community were often substandard, and most tribespeople lacked indoor plumbing and other amenities.

When our Chief [Ross Swimmer] developed systemic cancer . . . he asked me if I would attend some meetings in Washington and do some things that I don't normally do. And when he became well and thought about running for election again in 1983, he asked me if I would run for Deputy Chief with him, and I did.[75]

She faced problems, however, being a woman in a male-dominated culture:

I expected people to challenge me because I had an activist background, or challenge me because I was going around talking about something called grass roots democracy, and because my [future] husband and I were organizing these rural communities, and so I thought people would challenge me on my ideas when I began to run for election in 1983, but they didn't. The only thing people wanted to talk about in 1983 was my being a woman. That was the most hurtful experience I've ever been through. I would go to a meeting and no one wanted to talk about anything except the fact that I was female. Some people felt that we would be the laughing stock of all the tribes if we had a woman who was in the second highest position in the tribe.[76]

Some people were so opposed, in fact, that a campaign billboard with Mankiller's picture on it was burned down three times, and she received death threats in the mail. Despite these problems, Mankiller campaigned on the issues and was elected.

As deputy chief, Mankiller was the second-highest ranked official in the Cherokee Nation. In 1985 Chief Swimmer was offered a job with the BIA in Washington, D.C. When he accepted, Mankiller became the first female chief of the Cherokee Nation in modern history.

Mankiller's elevation to chief garnered intense media coverage. The attention gave her a chance to broadcast her positive message about Native American people, their traditions, their history, and their contributions to the United States.

In 1986 Mankiller and Charlie Soap were married. That same year she was elected to the Oklahoma Women's Hall of Fame and was honored as the American Indian Woman of the Year. She received an honorary doctorate from the University of New England and a citation for outstanding leadership from Harvard University.

In 1987 Mankiller ran for reelection. She ran against three well-regarded male candidates, but by focusing on issues instead of gender, Mankiller won by a generous margin. Again, the media celebrated her victory. She was elected Newsmaker of the Year by Women in Communications, voted one of the Women of the Year by *Ms.* magazine, and was featured in a special edition published by *Newsweek* called "Celebration of Heroes."

Mankiller Today

Mankiller experienced more health problems in 1990. One of her kidneys failed, but she received a transplanted kidney that was donated by her brother, Louis Donald Mankiller. In a matter of weeks she was back at work. In 1991 Mankiller was elected for her second full term in office, this time with a stunning 83 percent of the vote.

In 1994 the forty-eight-year-old Mankiller announced that,

Chief Mankiller meets with President Ronald Reagan in 1988 to discuss issues concerning Native Americans.

President Bill Clinton places the Presidential Medal of Freedom around the neck of Wilma Mankiller, recognizing her accomplishments within the Cherokee Nation.

because of her continuing health problems, she had decided not to run for reelection. "My season here is coming to an end,"[77] she said. During her time in office, the tribe opened three rural health care facilities, started a program to combat drug abuse, and expanded its Head Start program.

Although she was no longer running the day-to-day affairs of her tribe, Mankiller continued to remain in the limelight. In 1996 after ending her service as principal chief of the Cherokee, she became the visiting professor of Native American studies at Dartmouth College. In January 1998 President Bill Clinton presented Mankiller with the Presidential Medal of Freedom, the nation's highest civilian honor. Later in 1998 Mankiller required another kidney transplant, from which she recovered quickly. This time the donor was her niece, Virlee Williamson.

Mankiller's rise from poverty to become one of the most famous and powerful Native American women in the United States is a story full of struggle, sadness, joy, and great success. Mankiller proved that, in spite of hardship and adversity, Native American people still have much to teach the rest of the world. Mankiller affirmed this in her 1991 inaugural speech:

> It's time for a celebration because as we approach the twenty-first century, the Cherokee Nation still has a strong, viable tribal government. Not only do we have a government that has continued to exist, we have a tribal government that's growing and progressing and getting stronger. We've managed not just to barely hang on, we've managed to move forward in a very strong, affirmative way. . . . I think it's a testament to our tenacity, both individually and collectively as a people, that we've been able to keep the Cherokee Nation . . . going since time immemorial.[78]

NOTES

Introduction: Native American Leaders
1. Luther Standing Bear, *Land of the Spotted Eagle.* 1933. Reprint, Lincoln, NE: Bison Book Printing, 1978, p. 132.
2. Thomas H. Flaherty, ed., *The Mighty Chieftains.* Alexandria, VA: Time-Life Books, 1993, p. 10.

Chapter 1: The First Americans
3. Mari Sandoz, *Crazy Horse: The Strange Man of the Oglalas.* 1942. Reprint, Omaha: University of Nebraska Press, 1961, pp. 3–4.
4. Wilma Mankiller and Michael Wallis, *Mankiller: A Chief and Her People.* New York: St. Martin's Press, 1993, pp. 16–17.
5. Quoted in Jason Hook, *American Indian Warrior Chiefs.* New York: Sterling, 1989, p. 146.
6. James A. Maxwell, ed., *America's Fascinating Indian Heritage.* Pleasantville, NY: Reader's Digest Associates, 1978, p. 242.
7. Standing Bear, *Land of the Spotted Eagle,* pp. 193–94.
8. Standing Bear, *Land of the Spotted Eagle,* p. 196.
9. Standing Bear, *Land of the Spotted Eagle,* p. xxvii.
10. Alvin M. Josephy Jr., *500 Nations.* New York: Alfred A. Knopf, 1994, p. 430.
11. Quoted in Josephy, *500 Nations,* p. 431.
12. Standing Bear, *Land of the Spotted Eagle,* p. 231.
13. Quoted in Maxwell, *America's Fascinating Indian Heritage,* p. 242.

Chapter 2: King Philip
14. Quoted in David Horowitz, *The First Frontier: The Indian Wars and America's Origins, 1607–1776.* New York: Simon & Schuster, 1978, p. 17.
15. Quoted in Horowitz, *The First Frontier,* p. 18.
16. Flaherty, *The Mighty Chieftains,* p. 11.
17. Benjamin Church, *Diary of King Philip's War, 1675–1676.* Chester, CT: Pequot Press, 1975, p. 23.
18. Quoted in Church, *Diary of King Philip's War, 1675–1676,* pp. 26–27.
19. Quoted in Church, *Diary of King Philip's War, 1675–1676,* pp. 27–28.
20. Quoted in Horowitz, *The First Frontier,* p. 64.
21. Church, *Diary of King Philip's War, 1675–1676,* p. 79.

22. Quoted in Flaherty, *The Mighty Chieftains,* p. 15.
23. Quoted in Horowitz, *The First Frontier,* p. 73.
24. Quoted in Horowitz, *The First Frontier,* p. 74.
25. Quoted in Flaherty, *The Mighty Chieftains,* p. 16.
26. Quoted in Horowitz, *The First Frontier,* p. 82.

Chapter 3: Chief Pontiac

27. Flaherty, *The Mighty Chieftains,* p. 19.
28. Flaherty, *The Mighty Chieftains,* p. 20.
29. Quoted in Howard H. Peckham, *Pontiac and the Indian Uprising.* New York: Russell & Russell, 1947, p. 60.
30. Quoted in Peckham, *Pontiac and the Indian Uprising,* p. 62.
31. Quoted in Horowitz, *The First Frontier,* pp. 184–85.
32. Flaherty, *The Mighty Chieftains,* p. 25.
33. Quoted in Peckham, *Pontiac and the Indian Uprising,* pp. 237–38.
34. Quoted in Peckham, *Pontiac and the Indian Uprising,* pp. 238–39.

Chapter 4: Geronimo

35. Geronimo, *Geronimo's Story of His Life.* Ed., S. M. Barrett. New York: Duffield, 1906, p. 24.
36. Geronimo, *Geronimo's Story of His Life,* p. 31.
37. Geronimo, *Geronimo's Story of His Life,* p. 34.
38. Geronimo, *Geronimo's Story of His Life,* p. 36.
39. Angie Debo, *Geronimo: The Man, His Time, His Place.* Norman: University of Oklahoma Press, 1976, pp. 30–31.
40. Geronimo, *Geronimo's Story of His Life,* pp. 38–39.
41. Geronimo, *Geronimo's Story of His Life,* pp. 43–44.
42. Geronimo, *Geronimo's Story of His Life,* p. 45.
43. Geronimo, *Geronimo's Story of His Life,* p. 46.
44. Geronimo, *Geronimo's Story of His Life,* p. 52.
45. Geronimo, *Geronimo's Story of His Life,* p. 57.
46. Geronimo, *Geronimo's Story of His Life,* p. 63.
47. Geronimo, *Geronimo's Story of His Life,* p. 115.
48. Geronimo, *Geronimo's Story of His Life,* p. 118.
49. Quoted in Flaherty, *The Mighty Chieftains,* p. 105.
50. Quoted in Flaherty, *The Mighty Chieftains,* p. 105.
51. Quoted in Hook, *American Indian Warrior Chiefs,* pp. 181–82.
52. Geronimo, *Geronimo's Story of His Life,* p. 147.
53. Geronimo, *Geronimo's Story of His Life,* p. 215.

Chapter 5: Crazy Horse

54. Quoted in Russell Freedman, *The Life and Death of Crazy*

Horse. New York: Holiday House, 1996, p. 3.

55. Quoted in Sandoz, *Crazy Horse,* p. 118.
56. Sandoz, *Crazy Horse,* p. 221.
57. Sandoz, *Crazy Horse,* p. 253.
58. Sandoz, *Crazy Horse,* p. 287.
59. Quoted in Freedman, *The Life and Death of Crazy Horse,* p. 114.
60. Quoted in Freedman, *The Life and Death of Crazy Horse,* p. 120.
61. Quoted in Edward and Mabell Kadlecek, *To Kill an Eagle: Indian Views on the Last Days of Crazy Horse*. Boulder, CO: Johnson Books, 1981, pp. 117–18.

Chapter 6: Wilma Mankiller
62. Mankiller and Wallis, *Mankiller,* pp. 32–33.
63. Mankiller and Wallis, *Mankiller,* p. 36.
64. Mankiller and Wallis, *Mankiller,* p. 66.
65. Mankiller and Wallis, *Mankiller,* p. 69.
66. Quoted in Anita Merina, "Wilma Mankiller: Destined to Lead," *NEA Today*, October 1994, p. 7.
67. Wilma Mankiller, "Rebuilding the Cherokee Nation," *Gifts of Speech,* April 2, 1993. http://gos.sbc.edu/m/mankiller. html.
68. Mankiller and Wallis, *Mankiller,* p. 152.
69. Mankiller and Wallis, *Mankiller,* p. 157.
70. Mankiller, "Rebuilding the Cherokee Nation."
71. Mankiller and Wallis, *Mankiller,* p. 193.
72. Mankiller and Wallis, *Mankiller,* p. 205.
73. Mankiller and Wallis, *Mankiller,* p. 226.
74. Mankiller and Wallis, *Mankiller,* pp. 233–34.
75. Mankiller, "Rebuilding the Cherokee Nation."
76. Mankiller, "Rebuilding the Cherokee Nation."
77. Quoted in *Time*, "Milestones," April 18, 1994.
78. Mankiller and Wallis, *Mankiller,* p. 255.

Benjamin Capps, *The Great Chiefs*. Alexandria, VA: Time-Life Books, 1975. A big, colorful book rich in details concerning nineteenth-century Native American chiefs.

Thomas H. Flaherty, ed., *The Mighty Chieftains*. Alexandria, VA: Time-Life Books, 1993. A book that discusses the lives of Native American chiefs, ranging from Pontiac in the eighteenth century to the warrior chiefs of the Great Plains in the late nineteenth century. The book is illustrated with dozens of paintings, photographs, and maps.

Russell Freedman, *The Life and Death of Crazy Horse*. New York: Holiday House, 1996. A book about the life and death of Crazy Horse, illustrated with drawings from Amos Bad Heart Bull, a Sioux artist who was the nephew of He Dog, a cousin of Crazy Horse.

Geronimo, *Geronimo's Story of His Life*. Ed., S. M. Barrett. New York: Duffield, 1906. This is the story of Geronimo's life, as told by the Apache chief himself. This book offers a touching and poetic look at Apache life in the American Southwest in the nineteenth century, and it is an excellent choice of reading for anyone interested in Indian history.

Jason Hook, *American Indian Warrior Chiefs*. New York: Sterling, 1989. A book illustrated with many drawings, photos, and maps that discusses the life and times of Tecumseh, Crazy Horse, Chief Joseph, and Geronimo.

Edward and Mabell Kadlecek, *To Kill an Eagle: Indian Views on the Last Days of Crazy Horse*. Boulder, CO: Johnson Books, 1981. The book is based on interviews with over thirty Sioux elders who either knew Crazy Horse or had been told about him by older relatives. It is a fascinating work of living history that brings alive a man who died fighting for his people not so long ago.

Wilma Mankiller and Michael Wallis, *Mankiller: A Chief and Her People*. New York: St. Martin's Press, 1993. The inspirational and insightful autobiography of Wilma Mankiller. Besides recounting her fascinating life story, Mankiller explains three hundred years of Native American history.

Mankiller is a living resource for anyone who wants to learn more about the Cherokee people.

Luther Standing Bear, *Land of the Spotted Eagle.* 1933. Reprint, Lincoln, NE: Bison Book Printing, 1978. Luther Standing Bear was a Lakota Sioux who wrote this book in 1933 to tell others how the traditional Lakota lived. The book is full of personal reminiscences, including chapters on child rearing, the social organization of the Lakota, and the Native American religion. Standing Bear saves his most cutting words for the baffling behavior of the white people who subjugated his people.

Felix Sutton, *Indian Chiefs of the West.* New York: Julian Messner, 1970. A book about Crazy Horse, Chief Joseph, Sitting Bull, and other Indian chiefs of the West.

WORKS CONSULTED

Benjamin Church, *Diary of King Philip's War, 1675–1676*. Chester, CT: Pequot Press, 1975. A detailed eyewitness account of King Philip's War as written by an English army captain. A sympathetic, if somewhat dry, account of Native American life in seventeenth-century New England.

Angie Debo, *Geronimo: The Man, His Time, His Place*. Norman: University of Oklahoma Press, 1976. A detailed biography of Geronimo based both on the warrior's own words and on those of the men and women who knew him. The author is a student of Indian history and has written several books about Native Americans.

David Horowitz, *The First Frontier: The Indian Wars and America's Origins, 1607–1776*. New York: Simon & Schuster, 1978. This book offers an honest look at American history and emphasizes that the American frontier belonged to six hundred Native American tribes before it was "tamed" by white settlers. The book details the effect the French and English settlers and soldiers had on tribes, ranging from the Pilgrims to the American Revolution.

Alvin M. Josephy Jr., *500 Nations*. New York: Alfred A. Knopf, 1994. A lengthy book whose nearly five hundred pages discuss the entire history of Native Americans from the earliest years, when mastodons roamed the earth, to the last roundups for the reservations. It details Indian life from the Aztecs to the Iroquois to the tribes of the West using a fantastic array of paintings, photographs, and other visual aids.

Wilma Mankiller, "Rebuilding the Cherokee Nation," *Gifts of Speech*, April 2, 1993. http://gos.sbc.edu/m/mankiller.html. An amusing and thought-provoking speech given at Sweet Briar College in Virginia by Wilma Mankiller, the first female chief of the Cherokee in modern times. The speech was published on the Internet by Sweet Briar College.

James A. Maxwell, ed., *America's Fascinating Indian Heritage*. Pleasantville, NY: Reader's Digest Associates, 1978. A book that explores the first Americans, their customs, art, history, and how they lived. It is illustrated with dozens of drawings, photos, and other informative media.

Anita Merina, "Wilma Mankiller: Destined to Lead," *NEA Today*, October 1994. In this interview with a National Education Association reporter, Wilma Mankiller discusses the hardships she faced in school as a Cherokee Indian and her ideas for improving education for all students.

Howard H. Peckham, *Pontiac and the Indian Uprising.* New York: Russell & Russell, 1947. A book that brings to life the details of Pontiac and the Native American uprising that he fomented against the British. This book lists every battle of the revolt as well as many of the people who were involved in Pontiac's War.

Mari Sandoz, *Crazy Horse: The Strange Man of the Oglalas.* 1942. Reprint, Omaha: University of Nebraska Press, 1961. Much of what is known about Crazy Horse is based on interviews conducted by Mari Sandoz. In 1930 Sandoz interviewed the Oglala leader's surviving relatives and friends on the Pine Ridge Reservation. Sandoz used these interviews to reconstruct the life of Crazy Horse from the shadows of history. This book is an excellent source of information about the Sioux and their most famous leader.

Richard Slotkin and James Folsom, *So Dreadful a Judgment: An Anthology of Puritan Responses to King Philip's War, 1676–1677.* Middletown, CT: Wesleyan University Press, 1978. This book contains legal documents, essays, and other historic writings that detail the Puritans' response to King Philip and attempts by the Wampanoag Indians to regain their ancestral homelands.

Time, "Milestones," April 18, 1994. A short article about Wilma Mankiller's announcement not to run for reelection as chief of the Cherokee Nation.

INDEX

109

PICTURE CREDITS

ABOUT THE AUTHOR

Stuart A. Kallen is the author of more than 145 nonfiction books for children and young adults. He has written on topics ranging from the theory of relativity to rock-and-roll history to life on the American frontier. In addition, Mr. Kallen has written award-winning children's videos and television scripts. In his spare time, Stuart A. Kallen is a singer/songwriter/guitarist in San Diego, California.